PITCHING IN THE PROMISED LAND

PITCHING IN THE
PROMISED LAND

A STORY OF THE FIRST AND ONLY SEASON
IN THE ISRAEL BASEBALL LEAGUE

Aaron Pribble

UNIVERSITY OF NEBRASKA PRESS | LINCOLN AND LONDON

© 2011 by the Board of Regents of the
    University of Nebraska. All rights reserved.
Manufactured in the United States of America.

Library of Congress Cataloging-
    in-Publication Data
Pribble, Aaron, 1980–
    Pitching in the promised land: a
story of the first and only season in the
    Israel baseball league / Aaron Pribble.
p. cm. Includes bibliographical references.
    ISBN 978-0-8032-3472-7 (cloth: alk. paper)
1. Pribble, Aaron, 1980– 2. Jewish baseball
    players—Israel—Tel Aviv—Biography.
3. Baseball—Israel—Tel Aviv. I. Title.
    GV865.P75A3 2011
796.357092—dc22 [B]
    2010032735

Set in Janson by Bob Reitz.
    Designed by Nathan Putens.

For Mom and Dad
and Big Al, my little brother

And Abner said to Joab, "Let the young men now arise, and play before us." And Joab said, "Let them arise."

II Samuel 2:14

Contents

PITCHING IN THE PROMISED LAND

FIRST HALF

1 Five

"HAVE YOU EVER HAD A BAR MITZVAH?" BABIES cried in line behind me, adding undue stress to an already tense situation.

"A bar mitzvah? Um . . . no. Yes. No, not really." It was a strange question to be asked in the security line, especially from a young, heavily accented ticket lady.

"Well, which is it? Yes or no?" Both answers were correct in truth, depending on one's perspective, but that was not the sort of answer for which I surmised she was looking.

"Okay, no. No it is." Having previously answered a spate of rapidly fired questions—what is your name, what is your father's name, your mother's, your mother's mother's, where are you from, why are you going to Israel, how long will you be there, did you pack these bags, what's inside, why are you going to Israel again?—I thought I was doing well. But the steely eyes and measured, disdainful expression of my grand inquisitor indicated otherwise: wrong choice. Piqued, nervous, late for my flight, I tried to turn the tables. "What does it matter, anyway?" I asked in vain.

"Fine, *sank you*." The young official dismissively wrote a large "5" on my ticket, circled it, placed stickers with the same number on both my bags, and nudged me toward a separate station. I was instructed to empty the contents of my neatly packed luggage, which was searched and swabbed for explosives. Around me several families were engaged in the same process, the women wearing head scarves and several of the men speaking Arabic. The search was clean, thank goodness. On my way.

After a search of my person and an additional electronic search of my belongings, I eventually made it to the terminal, where I discovered the vast majority of people waiting previously in the snaked ticket line behind me already seated comfortably, waiting to board.

"Man." I sat down with a thud and exhaled loudly.

"Tsk, tsk, tsk," I heard someone tongue-click beside me. It was a middle-aged Israeli mother holding a young, fussy baby. She pointed to the neon-green sticker on one of my bags. "Five. That means you are not Jewish," she said with a bit of mischief in her eyes. "And this is why you are just now arriving to the terminal. Do not worry—you have not missed much." She smiled and I smiled back.

"But I am Jewish," I said. "Well . . . sort of."

"What do you mean, *sort of*? You are either Jewish or you're not, no?" Over the loudspeaker a plastic voice announced the commencement of preboarding, and the woman began to stand up, baby in the crook of her arm.

"It's a long story," I declared. "Have a nice flight."

In the air I had ample time to ponder the significance of being labeled a Five. Born to a Jewish mother and Christian father, a sort of redneck Jew-boy, I was technically part of the tribe. Even if I struggled to recite the Hanukkah prayer from memory and didn't go to temple for Yom Kippur, I was still a Jew, not a Five.

Five

No airport security lady should be able to tell me otherwise. And even if I was a Five, who cares? This did not seem like sufficient evidence to warrant an extra search.

Already it was becoming clear that this summer was going to be as much about discovering who I was as a Jew as it was about exploring who I was as a baseball player. Flying, I realized, toward the intersection of both my religious and my athletic identities. At least that latter part of myself I was sure of. On second thought, it had been almost two years since I'd played in a professional baseball game, and that was in France, no less. Perhaps I'd show up in Israel and they'd send me packing. Slap a sticker on my baseball bag that said NO GOOD. Just like the ticket lady. A Jew unsure or unconvinced of his heritage, I jumped on my average fastball, irregular slider, and decent change-up and rode them to the land of Abraham, the land of Moses and Muhammad, the land of vast deserts and clandestine oases, the land of occupations and cease-fires, the land of milk and honey, the land of Israel.

2 Kfar Hayarok

A Palestinian man was killed Monday at the volatile and closed border between Israel and Gaza after Palestinian gunmen opened fire on Israeli soldiers, officials said. The attack took place near the area where several hundred people trying to flee Gaza had been camped out and Israeli troops fired back.

New York Times, June 18, 2007

I AWOKE TO THE VOICE OF A YOUNG, FAUX-HAWKED flight attendant. "*Boqer tov*. Good morning, ladies and gentlemen. We are beginning our descent into Tel Aviv. Please put up your tray tables and return your seats to their upright position." Shifting awkwardly, groggy and disoriented, I took stock of the past twenty-four hours: a predawn northern California wake-up call, a San Francisco preflight religious interrogation, a Los Angeles layover, an Atlanta layover, thirteen further hours of air travel.

At the oily silver carousel I snatched my bags, hoisting one on each shoulder, and replayed the instructions in my head: someone will pick you up at the airport. Very specific. Departing baggage claim I laid eyes on a mass of humanity splayed across an oval security gate, assuredly awaiting newcomers of the Israel Baseball League (IBL). There were Sephardic families shouting and waiving, old Ashkenazi ladies gripping haute-couture handbags, off-duty members of the Israeli Defense Force (IDF) in green fatigues, an entourage of Hasidim, a television crew. Wow, I thought to myself. Walking forward into the mass of people, trying to appear proud yet humble, intentionally oblivious to the impending hysteria, I looked up and scanned the crowd, careful not to make any particular eye contact. In the distance I spotted a horizontal pad of yellow-lined legal paper. Scribbled in blue pen and written in all-caps, it read PRIBBLE. Though less than official, this seemed a relatively auspicious start. Passing the security-gate exit I feigned an aloof gait past the television crew who, it turned out, was not there to interview me. In fact, no one seemed to care. These thronging denizens of Ben-Gurion Airport were not here for the IBL at all. My welcome party would be much smaller.

Marty was the white-haired, bespectacled author of the impromptu sign. After we met, he and I negotiated a byzantine rental-car transaction before driving circuitously if not dangerously to our destination. Arriving at Kfar Hayarok (Green Village), Marty and I pulled up to a security gate, where two guards motioned us through. We passed a sign with an emblem of a large peacock and then headed in, seeking the league's facilities. Someone who looked like a ballplayer was running shirtless in the opposite direction, so we forged ahead. The road led us to the left, away from all over-head lights. Down a small, dark slope the thoroughfare turned to gravel, dirt. Detecting a hint of what could only be described as cow manure, I cracked the window for a heavier whiff.

"Oooh . . . you smell that, Marty?"

"Yeah, cows."

"This has gotta be the wrong way, huh?"

"Yeah, probably so. Let's turn around."

Instead, we unintentionally breached another dirt road, this time coming upon a horse stable. Behind it appeared what looked like a circus tent. This is fucking crazy—where are we?—I thought. After backing into a tree and running over a large rock en route to reversing toward the guard shack, we found the correct road and pulled up to a group of guys milling about.

7

"Is this the IBL?" Marty asked through a cracked window. The guy said yes and chuckled. Exiting our small European rental, the check-in was nowhere to be found, so we wandered over to some additional loiterers.

"Do you guys know how we check in for the IBL?" I asked.

"We're not sure, bro. There's no one really here."

"Oh, wait," said someone else. "There's Andrew. Talk to him."

A little fellow walked over wearing a flat-brimmed blue and red Dominican Republic baseball cap, slender chin-strap beard, faded blue polo, and sagging cargo shorts. Though he seemed at first blush to be a humble errand boy, Andrew was in charge of all league stats, the Web site, and, in these initial days, everything else involving player housing. When he spoke a confident, welcoming New York drawl revealed a character mature beyond his twenty-two years.

"Ay, man, how you doin'? I'll go get you a room. The thing is, we don't got too many beds right now. I'm in this room down the hall, but I'll get out 'cause I gotta move anyway."

After thanking Marty for the ride, I walked with Andrew down an open corridor revealing two bald heads doing shirtless pull-ups off a nearby overhang. Someone was taking dry hacks on the lawn, and others were smoking on a picnic table up several stairs. We exchanged obligatory head nods as I walked past.

Reaching the end of the hall, Andrew led me into the room, gathered up his stuff, and left. The space resembled a large broom closet, housing a dresser, a desk, and three beds consisting of wooden planks not quite six feet long by three feet wide, with a thin foam pad for support. This would not be a comfortable summer. I put a few things away and got ready for bed as the clock approached midnight. But I had just woken up. Great. Lying there restlessly, shins hanging off the edge of my wooden single, I thought of the implausible road that led me from teaching high school social studies in the Bay Area to playing in the inaugural season of the Israel Baseball League. It involved a chance encounter with my college baseball coach from Hawaii, a phone call to the IBL director of player development, and the good fortune of a season aligned perfectly with my summer break.

And I thought about my boyhood dream. Having played some independent and international ball, I never pitched in a Major League organization, much less the Show. Never drafted, never signed as a free agent, never joined that elite fraternity of athletes. Though I could convince myself semantically of reaching some minimum threshold of professional baseball, in sober moments such as this I could not expunge the regret, the heartfelt remorse, of a dream unfulfilled.

Halfway around the world in a strange bed on a peculiar *kfar*, tossing and turning anxiously in the desert night, I had no idea what the rising sun, so infinitely far from arriving, would bring.

3 Tel Aviv Lightning

AFTER AN ENDLESS NIGHT, MORNING EVENTUALLY came. I felt like a self-conscious freshman on his first day of high school. Like I hoped I didn't have a pimple or wasn't wearing the wrong kind of jeans. On the one hand, I felt relatively secure with myself; after all, I wasn't playing for rent money or alimony. But on the other, I did not know a soul. Not a single player. In the multiple degrees of separation that arise in the fairly small collegiate and professional baseball community, not a single person with whom I had ever competed seemed to know anyone on any of the rosters. I liked to think of myself as an affable fellow, but as any incoming ninth grader will tell you, it's not always easy to make friends.

Leaving my room I entered the warm morning sun to wander around. Before anyone, I encountered the peacocks. They were everywhere, crisscrossing the grounds in sublime oblivion, squawking, fanning, reigning over the *kfar*, their palace a spacious, verdant hutch from which to come and go at leisure. The entrance sign now made sense: royal peacock, unofficial ruler of Kfar Hayarok, enter at your own risk.

Players walked by, and we exchanged what's-ups and head nods, but that was it. Since I arrived several days late due to my teaching schedule, other guys seemed to have already coalesced into cliques. Somebody pointed me up the road to the cafeteria, and as I walked in it felt like a high school lunch room. There was a dull ruckus, dishes and spoons clanging intermittently against the low hum of conversation. I grabbed a light-pink tray and some silverware and made my way down the buffet aisle, ending up with some cucumbers and cottage cheese, a typical Israeli breakfast. As I walked toward the crowd I was struck with a pang of anxiety. Several people stole glances in my direction. Where do I sit? Should I grab a seat by myself? I don't want anybody to think I'm a loner. Those guys over there look okay, but that's too big of a crowd.

I spotted an isolated straggler and plopped down next to him with a degree of hesitation. "What's up, man?" I initiated.

"Hey, what's up?" replied the muscular, blond-haired stranger.

"Aaron . . . Pribble," I said and extended my right hand.

"Jeff Hastings. Nice to meet you."

"Where you from?"

"New Hampshire."

"Oh, yeah? D'you play up there as well?"

"Yeah. I played for the Nashua Pride of the Atlantic League."

Oh, shit, I thought to myself. This guy must be good. That's the best independent league in the country.

"But that's during the summer only. During the year I'm a teacher and a coach."

Ha, nice. "I teach as well, but in the Bay Area in California." We had an instant connection. "I thought I had to be the only teacher here, but I guess not. So what team are you on?"

"The Tel Aviv Lightning."

"No shit? Me too. Sweet."

"Nice!" he replied with a large grin. "What position do you play?"

"I pitch. You?"

"I play right."

Cool. This guy will be great to have behind me.

After breakfast we walked around and began meeting other players (it's always easier with a buddy at your side). Jeff and I quickly discovered there were some bona fide characters in this league. We met Alan Gardner, a guy in his forties who had been practicing law for nearly twenty years. He got signed during a tryout but had three clients in jail. After he spoke with his charges and the judge, they all thought he should come play, so he put his criminal practice on hold and went to Israel. The oldest of the group was another New Yorker named Scott Cantor. In his fifties at least, he was a Pilates instructor and the last white guy to play in the Negro Leagues. At least this is what he told us. He might not have been as old as Moses, but in baseball terms he was pretty close. Upon meeting them I could not tell if they were studs or already put out to pasture, but time would tell. In addition, there was a Maori fellow, Moko, who didn't speak. Actually, he did speak, but exceedingly little. He would turn out to be one heck of a hitter.

And in the entire Israel Baseball League, there seemed to be just one Muslim—a Turk named Alper Ulutas, also from the Big Apple. Jeff and I heard a story about his incoming flight, not so very different from my own. Before the airport staff let him into the country he underwent a stiff, lengthy interrogation. They inquired into his reasons for the journey and asked him to recite as much of his family tree as he could recall, from his father several generations back. Where are you from? Why are you here? they asked him relentlessly. Finally, Al got fed up, rose from his chair, and said, "Man, I'm from *Brooklyn*." I guess that was good enough for them.

At some point Jeff and I found our way back to the living area, seated in front of the rooms on a centrally located stoop. As the weeks went by the stoop would become a familiar spot to pass time and listen to stories, but at this moment it was completely new.

Someone recounted the symbolic selection of Sandy Koufax as the last pick of the IBL draft. That he would come out of a forty-one-year retirement to pitch in the land of his forefathers, bless us with the presence of the greatest Jew to ever play the game. We heard a tale about some crazy Australian who got in an altercation on one of his first days in the country. He and some guys thought the cabbie was trying to shaft them on the fare, so they refused to pay but also wouldn't get out. When the cabbie came around to the back of the car this dude jumped in the front seat, locked the door, and wouldn't let him back in. But much to the dismay of the Aussie prankster and his unwitting accomplices, the cabbie had a gun. He pulled it, shouted incomprehensibly in Hebrew, and everyone ran.

Later that day the Dominicans arrived. They were a FORCE, all hanging together, speaking very little English, shrouded in mystery. It did not help that they had been housed separately from the other players toward the south end of the facilities, on a mini Hispaniola of their own. The IBL tryout in the Dominican Republic was rumored to have produced a deluge of incredible talent. Someone said, had it wanted to, the league could have filled its rosters entirely with Latin American players. In fact, teams were initially judged based on their number of Latinos, which would not turn out to be an entirely incorrect method of assessment. We heard of Maximo Nelson, a six-nine flamethrower who would still be with the Yankees had he not falsely claimed to be married to an American girl on his visa. There was Stuart Brito, who played first and third for the Dodgers' single-A team, and Raul Franco, who made it to double A with the Yankees. The latter two I recognized from the Tel Aviv roster. Good news. Then there was Angel Ramirez, who was rumored to have been the third-rated prospect with the Angels before lying about his age and getting into trouble with his visa. Finally Julio, the brother of Vladimir Guerrero, *the* Vladimir Guerrero, was here too. And these were just the guys we heard about on the stoop. There were plenty more to come. In total, nine different countries would be represented: Israel, the United States, the Dominican Republic, Colombia, Australia, New Zealand, Canada, Japan, and even the Ukraine. A veritable potpourri of religions, ethnicities, nationalities, and cultures.

That evening was our first meeting with the entire league. Everyone gathered in the cafeteria. The honorary commissioner, Dan Kurtzer, welcomed us and said how proud he was to be there, that this was truly a once-in-a-lifetime experience. With each passing word players grew increasingly excited, until the commissioner began talking about the code of conduct, which included being back at the *kfar* by midnight. Yeah, right. A list of league rules and punishments was even passed out, then promptly discarded.

Afterward it was time to meet our team. There was a Tel Aviv Lightning sign at a table near the back of the room, so Jeff and I made our way over. As we approached there were two Dominicans who, we guessed, were Franco and Brito. Stuart "Pupo" Brito was a mountain of a man, a bear. He had a big round face and bald head, big round ears, big round biceps, and enormous thighs. As intimidating as he seemed, however, his first smile gave him up: Brito was one big cub. I was glad to have him as our first baseman. Raul Franco, Frankie, was probably in his forties, though he claimed to be twenty-nine. His face revealed years of playing shortstop under the sun, and his head was topped with thinning cornrows. He moved slow, talked slow, and walked slow, a mellow guy.

Everyone else looked normal enough, except for one fellow wearing pajama pants and a Miami Heat jersey. He had a prominent yet handsome nose, and his head was accentuated by a mane of curly black hair à la the biblical Samson or Howard Stern. "That must be an Israeli," I whispered to Jeff.

"Must be."

He wasn't. Nathan Israel Bloomberg Fish (his full name) was a DJ, street artist, and youth baseball instructor currently living in New York who played ball at the University of Cincinnati. Kevin Youkilis, the big league Jew for the Red Sox, was his college roommate. Fish, as we called him, would be our third baseman. He exuded a leonine coolness, and I was immediately drawn to him, in spite of his outfit.

As we chatted, one particularly loud and gregarious teammate seemed to be everywhere at once, bouncing around among the others. Wearing loud board shorts, a tank top, and flip-flops, he held back his long surfer-blond hair with large bug-eyed sunglasses. His name was Dane Wigg, and he was the Aussie prankster who several days before was nearly shot dead by an incensed cabbie. Wiggy would be our catcher.

The squad was rounded out with two Israelis, a Canadian, another Australian, and several Americans to be named later. Our manager was Steve Hertz, a junior-college coach, Jew, and former big leaguer for the Colt 45s (now the Houston Astros). Skip, as we'd call him, displayed a mellow, unassuming veneer belying a ferociously competitive spirit. Sizing up our team, it was hard to tell if we'd be any good. Asking around, it seemed Franco, Brito, Jeff, and I were the only ones with professional experience, and mine was relatively limited. The rest of the guys had played various levels of college ball, and one, my roommate Joey, was rumored to have played only in high school. But he was a conservative Jew, and I guess that made up for it. The formula I began to decipher was this: to be a player in the IBL, one's talent was inversely related to his degree of Jewishness. On the one end, if you weren't Jewish at all, like Jeff or the Dominicans, you had to be *very* good. On the other, if you were Orthodox or, better yet, Israeli, I guessed all you needed was a heartbeat. According to that formulation I placed myself squarely in the middle of the talent pool: a half-assed Jew and half-assed former pro.

4 Opening Day

In the land of milk and honey, it is time for peanuts and hot dogs—the Israel Baseball League makes its debut Sunday night when the Petach Tikva Pioneers play host to the Modi'in Miracle. A high demand for tickets has moved organizers to double the seating capacity at the Yarkon Sports Complex to accommodate a projected 2,000 spectators expected to attend.

New York Times, June 23, 2007

IT WOULD NOT BE UNTIL OPENING DAY THAT WE had our first chance to see players in action and evaluate the league's talent. For several days we were marooned at the *kfar*, unable to practice on an actual baseball field, only one of which existed in the entire country, though we did not know this at the time. Everyone got creative, turning the soccer pitch into a diamond, the lawn near the satellite university into a batting cage, the road from the guard shack through the dorms to the horse stables into a track, and the rock quarry into a weight room.

In the morning I got up to throw with Adam Crabb, our tall, lanky pitcher from Adelaide, Australia. I had played in his hometown for a week in high school and immediately liked him. I liked him for his personality and his quirky yet competitive approach to the game. He was our team's first overall draft pick, and word on the street said he was dirty. Crabb stood six-four but dipped down to throw from somewhere between sidearm and three-quarters. Just playing catch with him I could tell he had a nasty slider that was only augmented by his unorthodox arm angle. The kicker, though, was his one-fingered fastball, just like a crab. Seriously. Instead of gripping the baseball with the middle and pointer fingers on top, he dropped his middle finger off the side of the ball and moved his thumb up the other end. Like he was throwing with only two pincers. It made the ball do some silly, often unpredictable things.

Since our first game was a few days away, after completing an improvised workout we got ready to head over to Israel's lone field for Opening Day. We were supposed to depart at half past two, but forty-five minutes later the buses arrived and twenty minutes after that we actually left. The departure time had apparently been moved back an hour, but only a handful of players were privy to this information. Thus far everything seemed to travel by word of mouth; no formal directions were given. The Netanya Tigers, for example, decided they would practice before the game, so the team got up early and found their own way to the yard. But upon arrival they were informed the field could not be used, that there was no time anyway, so they ended up moving chairs, picking up garbage, prepping for the game. This wasn't quite anarchy . . . more like intended telepathy. Something as simple as an announcement board in the cafeteria or the dorms would have been a step in the right direction.

Eventually we arrived at Ha Yarkon for Opening Day. Ha Yarkon Sports Complex was located in the small Baptist Village enclave named for its founding group of missionaries. It was hidden just off the main highway by tall grass and a ring of eucalyptus trees. Down a twisting gravel road, a smattering of plaster-white, Spanish-tiled dwellings formed a semicircle around baseball and softball fields, both of which were magnificently tailored. I guessed this was because many of the village's resident custodians hailed from the great state of Texas, where America's pastime is of religious importance. As shepherds of Yarkon Field they took their job very seriously. There was no swearing, no chewing of sunflower seeds, no littering. The field itself was perfect, highlighted by its austere surroundings. The grounds crew reminded me of those ascetic monks who brewed world-famous beer. Their rigid discipline, while exhausting, created an incredible product.

One piece of information that did reach the majority of players was to wear khaki shorts, uniform tops, and team hats. As I walked around in ninety-degree weather wearing black and turquoise Tel Aviv Lightning gear, I wondered how our team would play in such heat-sucking apparel. But since our first game wasn't for several days we hung around signing autographs, kissing babies.

An hour beforehand the atmosphere was a combination of joy and uncertainty. The *New York Times* was there, as well as CNN and Fox News. PBS was filming the game to be shown back in the States. People seemed genuinely happy to be there. One fellow was wearing a blue and gold jersey with "Israel" on the front and "Menorah 25" on the back. A son was being carried on his dad's shoulders holding a sign that read, "Dan Drori from the Modi'in Miracle Is My Uncle." Modi'in was playing the Petach Tikva Pioneers for this historic first game. It *was* historic. In spite of my proclivity for sarcasm, I knew something genuinely unique was taking place, that it was felt alike by players, league officials, families, and fans. It may have been more than just the start of a season.

An old man held up a sign that read, in descending order:

Jews returning to Israel: check.
Baseball in the Holy Land: check.
World Peace: _____

Before the game, players from all six teams assembled behind the first and third base lines. They announced the two teams playing, including the elder statesman Scotty Cantor for Petach. Jogging out to the field as they called his name, he grinned uncontrollably, the long-haired hippie of his youth emerging beneath the balding, weathered veneer of middle age. He was a kid again, if only for this moment. I loved him instantly. After we were all introduced, to hearty applause Commissioner Kurtzer threw out the first pitch. (At the time I did not know our fates would intertwine in this very spot after the championship game on the last day of the season.) Kurtzer's toss missed the catcher and hit the umpire, standing just to the right of home. Then some *macher*, some big shot, from the Diamondbacks threw out another. Though the Dominican ambassador to Israel as well as the chargé d'affaires of Australia were in attendance, they did not throw additional first pitches.

Next a young woman performed "Hatikva," the Israeli national anthem. We stood with our hats *on*, as was custom. Playing a keyboard just behind home plate, she sang with passion, behind each word, each syllable, a haunting strength:

> *In the Jewish heart a Jewish spirit still sings,*
> *And the eyes look east toward Zion*
> *Our hope is not lost,*
> *Our hope of two thousand years,*
> *To be free in our land,*
> *In the land of Zion and Jerusalem*

Hatikva in Hebrew means "the hope." The song's uplifting message, however, was belied by a slow cadence and solemn tenor. Though it was paradoxical, I thought maybe hope for a better future, grounded in a pragmatic if not pessimistic reality, was what "Hatikva" captured about the Israeli character. "Hatikva" also encapsulated our hope for this fledgling league. For the players, we wished the IBL would be successful so that it would further our own careers. Larry Baras and the rest of the founders hoped the game would be a positive contribution to the state.[1] More

---

1. Larry Baras was a Boston businessman famed for creating the cream cheese–filled bagel. He was even featured on the Food Network. Little did any of us know, it would be easier for Baras to inject cream cheese into a bagel than America's pastime into the Holy Land.

whimsically, perhaps baseball could help add a "check" to the last box on the old man's sign; maybe baseball *could* contribute to peace in the region. It was already rumored that the Kingdom of Jordan was starting a league in the upcoming year. If the IBL was successful, baseball could spread to Gaza and the West Bank. From there anything would be possible.

The first pitch came just before sundown. As the dying light of evening fell gently against the desert, casting a rosy hue upon the grass and sand, Matt Bennett, a formidable lefty from Australia, delivered a strike for Modi'in at the knees. After that it was baseball as usual, albeit with a Jewish twist. Over the PA system after the second pitch, the announcer exclaimed, "Sam Weinberg, please report to the scorers' table. Your son Yehuda is here."

During the game we chatted, walked around. The league gave us Sharpies, and we signed scores of autographs. My roommate Joey, who was not a day over nineteen, had just signed his first. "Wait, take a picture of this!" he said to a friend. It's always nice to get an ego boost, but this was a bit much. Youngsters were coming up to us three, four, five times. They didn't know who we were, just wanted more scribbles on balls, gloves, bats, arms, backs of shirts. Later Joey came up to me excitedly. "Aaron, I just signed some girl's ass!" It was getting out of hand.

In addition to the kids, young ladies were also clamoring for attention; several were mesmerized in romantic awe. One roundish dishwater blonde with tattooed ankles was inseparable from several Dominicans who did not seem to mind. Other women were more interested in being photographed with players, inevitably receiving an arm around the shoulder or a hand on the back. They had no idea what the game was about, simply basking in the ostensible fame. Though none of us deserved it, we felt like heroes, champions. A far cry from teaching third-period social studies less than one month earlier.

The final score was 9–1, Modi'in. Matt Bennett threw all seven innings for a complete-game victory (games were two innings shorter than in Major League Baseball). He was absolutely dominating. The Pioneers' only run came on a blast by Ryan Crotin, a Hulk-like outfielder from upstate New York, in the fourth inning. After the game players and coaches from both teams were mobbed. The atmosphere was frenetic, nearly out of control. It was the first time such an event had happened in this country, in this part of the world, and people did not know how to respond.

In the main fans cheered at strikeouts, big hits, and great plays. They stood up for the fifth-inning stretch, sang a Hebrew-English mix of "Take Me Out to the Ball Game," and ate their fair share of kosher hot dogs. It looked like this thing was going to catch on here after all. That is, if no one got hurt.

5 Safety First

After the game there was a bit of an incident. We were sitting down to a late dinner in the caf when Modi'in and Petach Tikva arrived. One of Petach's brawny infielders entered, screaming passionately: "That was fucking bullshit! We could have all been killed! You know how many bomb threats they get a day here? We're in the Middle East. There are *terrorists*. I'm fucking leaving. It's not safe. I'm outta here."

Someone from Modi'in disagreed rather petulantly: "No, they *don't*. Chill out, dude."

"Oh yeah? Chill out? They steal my glove, and you want me to chill? Come here. I'll fucking kick your ass."

"Whoa. Easy, man. Calm down."

"My coach gave me that glove, and he died this year! I'll rip your fucking head off if you think I'm joking."

"Hey, I didn't know. Just cool off, okay?"

The glove would be returned to the infielder in the caf moments later. A teammate had stashed the glove in a hatbox so it wouldn't get swiped when the teams were bum-rushed by fans after the game, but the infielder had no idea.

His claim wasn't completely unfounded, however, since several guys' bats and batting gloves were stolen during the chaos. The infielder was clearly upset about losing his mitt, and rightfully so, but while on-field security could have been improved, this incident was a far cry from terrorism. As unreasonable as this claim may have been, many players agreed that the risk was too high. Some were uneasy about playing, and a few were genuinely concerned about going to the field the next day. One player from another team actually left for home shortly thereafter.

"What if a terrorist had a bomb?" I heard several players utter.

"Yeah, there would have been no one to stop him."

The terrorism comment seemed a bit untenable, but there was a point to be made about security. They probably should have done a better job checking people as they came in, but you couldn't, you shouldn't, isolate everyone in attendance. In Israel *shuks* and farmers' markets abound; the only difference was here there were armed guards checking people coming in and out. A setup like this would probably make sense for the league. How many times, I wondered, had I worried about getting blown up at a game? Never. It was the type of thing that could happen only when you paired baseball and the Middle East.

Nonetheless, in response to the cafeteria blowup in particular and a perceived lack of safety at Opening Day more generally, Commissioner Kurtzer and Ami Baran talked with us about security the following day. Ami was a leading figure in Israeli baseball and softball. The IBL director of Israeli operations, he was also chosen as the league's only native manager. An Israeli Police Force major, Ami took a leave of absence this summer in order to coach. With his shaved head and dark sunglasses, it was easy to picture Ami as a member of Mossad or Special Forces. Except for the large black leather fanny pack he carried, Ami looked tough.

"Guys, you should know that the *kfar* is very well protected. Here you are quite safe. But . . ." There was a long pause in which players moved to the edge of their seats. In some ways the fact that the security issue was being addressed at all validated their earlier claims and assertions. ". . . you need to know that this group is a target. Think about it: a large number of Americans living in a central location who have started to get some publicity. You may not be a high-profile target, but there are people who might know you are here."

Shit. Perhaps I had erred in not taking the issue more seriously. The league *had* recently received a fair amount of media attention, and if something were to happen it would surely make national and international news.

"So, there are some things you can do to be safe," he continued. "Look out for suspicious bags. Be aware of things that seem out of place. Most importantly, look out for each other." These were general tips, but I supposed they made sense. There was a guard shack and a large yellow iron gate at the front of the grounds, though the laissez-faire sentries did not look very imposing. As I had discovered on a run several days ago, there were multiple points of entry into the *kfar*, and someone who really wanted to get in would have no trouble doing so. But following a few commonsense guidelines certainly could not hurt.

I guessed Ami and Commissioner Kurtzer wished to allay our concerns, but I still felt ambivalent. Maybe security was a big issue, maybe not. I think most players felt the same way. Looking over at the Petach Tikva infielder and his followers, their fears seemed to be somewhat assuaged. Either way, at each game the rest of the season we were promised there would be bag checks and security personnel. It was hoped there would be no more stolen gloves. Personally, I wasn't going to change my routine in order to keep safe. I was just ready to pitch. We'd been here for nearly a week, and the Lightning had yet to see the field. It was time for us to play ball.

6 Call from the Pen

THE *ISRAELI* WAS STARTING OUR FIRST GAME? WHAT crap. At least start the number-one pick, Crabb, or maybe that young kid from Emory who seemed to have good stuff. If Skip didn't want to give me the nod, at least one of these guys should get it. We had had a practice so everyone could be evaluated, and though I didn't see the Israeli throw, I figured he couldn't have much. But maybe Skip was making a deft PR move, starting the local guy in front of the hometown fans. Though I wasn't happy, it seemed best to give Skip the benefit of the doubt, for now.

The Israeli, Dan Rothem, made it safely through the first two innings. In the third he faltered, giving up three quick runs while recording two laborious outs. To be honest I didn't think he had bad stuff. His mechanics were clean, he had a nice release, and he could throw his breaking pitches for strikes.

We were conversing in the dugout about Ra'anana's green and yellow uniforms. They looked like the Oakland A's. Their logo was a yellow *resh*, the Hebrew letter *r*, a mirror image of our own. But on their hats it looked like a banana, so we began calling them the Ranana Bananas.

"Pribble, get loose." I didn't expect Skip to have such a short leash. Jumping from the bench, I grabbed my glove and headed to the bullpen. I threw a few pitches and then looked back toward the dugout. Skip tumbled his pointer fingers end over end, the universal sign for GET HOT. There was a runner on second, and Rothem was behind the hitter 2-0. I threw a few more pitches and looked back. A lefty was on deck. Whatever happens to this guy, Skip's gonna want to match me up with the next hitter, I thought, lefty on lefty. Rothem threw a strike for 2-1. Then the next pitch squibbed all the way to the backstop, moving the runner to third and bringing the count to 3-1. I threw a few more pitches. Bursting with adrenaline, not having pitched in relief since Mississippi four years prior, I couldn't quite tell if I was loose. Ball four. The hitter jogged to first, and Skip and Wiggy, catching, walked to the mound. I threw another pitch. Turning again toward the field my eyes caught Skip stick out his left hand and point to the pen, taking the ball from Rothem and patting him on the butt. I flipped my baseball to the dirt, adjusted my hat, and looked up to see Yarkon Field brightly illuminated against the night sky. There were about three hundred people in attendance, less than the thousands for Opening Day but still respectable. It seemed the lights were like giant magnifying glasses, focusing everyone's attention on the meeting in the middle of the diamond.

I began to jog from beyond the outfield, past shortstop, to the infield grass. Well, here you go, I thought. Hope you have your stuff. Three years later and you're doing it again. All those afternoons spent running and throwing after school, telling your students about that crazy league halfway around the world. Now here you are: pitching in the Promised Land. No more excuses. Let's see if you still got it.

My mind was racing when I finally approached the mound. But

as I walked up the dirt slope to meet Rothem, Skip, and Wigg, my thoughts faded away. "Good job, Dan," I said as Rothem walked to the dugout.

"All right, mate. Let's do this!" said Wiggy with a large peppy grin.

Skip handed me the ball. "Okay, Aaron, lots of strikes."

As directed, the first pitch was a strike but covered way too much of the plate. Luckily, the lefty was taking. Wigg called for another fastball, which I tried to guide toward the inside corner. I released it early, and the ball sailed up and in, nearly hitting the batter. The next pitch, a slider, missed low and away, moving the count to 2-1. With runners on first and third, already down three, it was an important situation. A base hit would bring in at least one and put another runner in scoring position.

When Wiggy wiggled four fingers, calling for a change-up, I was a bit surprised. True, the hitter would be looking fastball, ahead in the count with runners on, but another ball would mean one pitch away from loading the bases. The change was my best pitch, but I didn't think Wigg knew that, having seen it only once in warmups. It was a ballsy call. Let's do it, I thought. Throw it with good arm speed, and the guy will juice up, swing right through. He did, 2-2. Unfortunately, now the hitter had seen all my pitches. I had nothing left with which to surprise him. Two strikes, lefty on lefty, he'd probably be looking for the slider since I missed with it earlier. So Wiggy put down one finger, and I nodded. It was a good fastball, away at the knees, and the hitter swung over the top for strike three. Our dugout cheered as I walked gratefully off the field. Getting that first one out of the way was a nice feeling.

After a few quiet innings, Jeff, Fish, Franco, and Brito came out swinging in the bottom of the third. Filling out the heart of our lineup, they could score runs in a hurry. I hoped we would be able to pitch okay, because our offense was just fine. In the end I finished the game, and we came back to win 9–3. Striking out seven hitters, exceeding expectations, I didn't give up a hit. Though my velocity wasn't great, the change was spot-on, forcing swing-throughs all night. It was apparent this is what needed to happen if I wished to have any success this season.

It was nice to get Tel Aviv's first-ever win, but in the moment I neglected to take the game ball for my dad. You could mark the stages of my life with baseballs I'd given him: Little League, high school, college, independent, international ball. I knew he treasured the gesture, and I enjoyed making him happy. It would have been nice to spend this moment together; I'd just have to let him know as much another time.

I went out after the game with Rothem, due only slightly to the fact that he had a car while everyone else rode the bus. We ended up at a coffee shop on Dizengoff Street in Tel Aviv, discussing our approaches to specific Ra'anana hitters. Eventually the conversation turned to the league and then our lives more generally. I learned the subject of my criticism hours earlier was in fact the first of only two Israelis to play Division I baseball in the United States. A college coach staged a camp in Israel when Dan was a boy, and when he grew up he made the coach's Georgia Southern University team, later transferring to Gardner-Webb in North Carolina—a Jewish Israeli playing for a Baptist school in the Deep South, a spectacle nearly as peculiar as the IBL itself. After that he got a job working for a nonprofit focusing on the Israeli-Arab conflict, established by Danny Abraham, the founder of Slim-Fast. Principled and bright, Rothem's political and religious beliefs were influenced by the leftist upbringing of his parents, both of whom were raised on a kibbutz before moving to Tel Aviv prior to Dan's birth. And since he was a secular Israeli, it was clear Rothem would *not* be going with us on our first leaguewide adventure several days later to that epicenter of religion and faith, Jerusalem.

7 Al Quds

At least 11 Palestinian militants and 2 civilians were killed Wednesday during Israeli raids in Gaza in the deadliest day of fighting since the Islamic militant group Hamas took control there nearly two weeks ago.

New York Times, June 28, 2007

THAT PLAYER WHO WENT HOME A FEW DAYS AGO was from Ra'anana. He said it was because he didn't like it here, but we guessed it was because he was scared. Either way, he was about to miss out on our first leaguewide adventure. When we piled into buses just after daybreak to head for Jerusalem, security and baseball were far from our thoughts.

It was a benevolent gesture. We were owed nothing but the terms of our contract, but league founder Larry Baras wanted the players to experience this ancient land, not simply play ball for two months and return home. I was grateful. The IBL chartered two buses, hired a couple of guides, and packed lunch to feed an army. Surprisingly, not everyone went. Some guys were too hung over, and others were just too lazy. When I inquired about why so few Dominicans came along, Fish mentioned something vague about a lack of money.

Yesterday there was a minor hubbub when we did not receive our first check. Some guys were complaining that they had already run out of money. I wanted to tell them to visit the bars less. Our first time getting paid, it was understandable that there should be some logistical difficulties. I was fine waiting a few days, seemed the least we could do for the league, especially in light of what it was doing for us.

As we were about to leave for Jerusalem—known to Muslims as Al Quds, meaning "the Holy"—Larry boarded our bus. He wished us a good trip and said he was happy we were able to share in this experience. Larry then addressed the money issue, explaining that financial transactions in Israel had proved more difficult than he had imagined, especially on Shabbat, the one day a week when we did not play, when nobody in the country seemed to do a thing. Since no banks were open on the Day of Rest, which began at varying times Friday afternoon and ended at sundown Saturday, he had spent Friday morning traversing Tel Aviv in search of a solution. To make matters worse, some players wanted shekels, some dollars, others checks, and he had tried to accommodate everybody. Originally, he planned to pay everyone two thousand shekels—five hundred bucks—for the first two weeks because he thought this was the easiest method. However, players complained the exchange rate was closer to 4.1 or 4.2 than 4.0, said they wanted either more money or to be paid in cash, which was understandable considering the contract stipulated U.S. dollars. Whatever. Larry eventually decided that players could get paid as they wanted; in the future they just had to let him know. Because of the difficulties this time, he asked for a little patience and said we'd be remunerated shortly. He even told us that at one point he was running around the city with sixty thousand dollars in a briefcase, trying to figure out what to do.

I perceived Larry to be a good person, his heart in the right place. I knew people were working hard and it was difficult creating a league from scratch, especially in a foreign country. Some guys definitely needed to complain less. Talking trash was okay as long as it was eventually refined into something constructive for the league. We joked that everything would finally get figured out in the eighth week, just as we were ready to leave. Little did we know, it would not.

On the ride to Jerusalem the majority of the bus was asleep. We awoke to the sight of a large Mecca-to-Elvis statue exalting a pit stop one would find along any major U.S. highway, overlooking the valley below. Buttressed by a gas station, diner, and gift shop stood two large plaster statues of the King, reminiscent of the cover of *Elvis in Jerusalem*, a book by Tom Segev about American influence in Israel. We disembarked, noshed, micturated, explored the simulated weirdness of the place.

Boarding again, the bus driver swung his fist in the air, garbling incomprehensibly at one of the straggling players, his accent so thick we could barely understand him. "You're out! You too late," he repeated, grinning, ". . . getting on the bus." His attempt at baseball humor was a pleasant surprise. Players chuckled, though it was unclear if the laughs were directed at the bussie himself.

Winding down Road 1 we arrived in Jerusalem minutes later. Nearly twenty-four hundred feet high, elevated in the cool and breezy hills, the clime was much preferable to muggy Tel Aviv. Our first stop was a vista point near the Mount Scopus Forest, which was more like a hill dotted intermittently with trees. North and south in the hazy foreground, in varying shades of tan, lay Samaria, Judea, Palestine, or the West Bank, depending on one's cultural narrative. A small line snaked across several hills, which I quickly recognized as the Wall of Separation. From this vantage point the partition seemed small and innocuous. Behind it was Ramallah, one of the largest Palestinian towns, as well as Ma'ale Adumim, one of the largest Israeli settlements. I hoped I would make it to the former this summer, but had no interest in visiting the latter, which in my view was an unjust, overt impediment to the peace process.

Our guide, a stout Israeli lady, plucked an olive branch from a nearby tree, holding it up as a symbol of goodwill, sermonizing about the importance of coexistence and mutual respect. If Israel continued building settlements, I wanted to tell her, peace would be a long time coming. I picked a small branch nonetheless and tucked it in my pocket. Out of the corner of my eye I saw a player sneak behind a rocky outcropping and pee. It was time to go.

On the bus again we drove to the Mount of Olives, the site of a massive Jewish cemetery and Jesus's ascension to heaven, overlooking the Old City. Once there, one of the Colombian pitchers, Rafael, immediately jumped on a tourist-friendly camel, yipping and yelling as we took pictures.

"*Vamos, caballero! Vamos!*" the Arabic jockey shouted at Rafael.

In the distance the gold Dome of the Rock glistened prominently, built upon the holiest, most contentious rock in the world. It was a rock in this very mosque that Abraham is said to have been willing to sacrifice his son for God, the same rock from which Muhammad is believed to have ascended to heaven hundreds of years later. The same rock over which the Jews' most holy of temples had been built, then destroyed, then built again, then destroyed once more, the remnants of which now constituted the Western Wall, the holiest location in Judaism. The same rock, the most hallowed of places for Jews and Muslims alike. Descendants of Abraham's son Isaac, Jews say, "We were here first!" Descendants of Abraham's son Ishmael, Muslims say, "We're here now!" From one man, one rock, a fratricidal progeny since time immemorial, reverberating through the present, into the future. The same rock.

On the bus again we reached a bazaar overflowing with religious and secular tchotchkes alike. There were hookahs and swords, statues of Jesus, Jewish cookbooks. For me and my passionately progressive mother I bought two pins, each with Palestinian and Israeli flags joined at the center, worn by various leaders at various stages of the peace process. Corny though it may have been, I hoped one day these two states would be connected on earth as they were on these small bronze brooches.

On the bus again, we stopped at the Church of All Nations.

On the bus again, we stopped and ate lunch in a park.

On the bus again, we reached the Old City. Finally.

Visiting the Western Wall, wearing paper *kippas* when without their own, players stuffed notes between cracks of Jerusalem stone. We went to King David's Tomb and the Church of the Holy Sepulcher, where Jesus was crucified, buried. Since it was Shabbat very little was open, save for the Muslim Quarter, which was rocking. We ventured in. It smacked of pure commerce, not an inch of available space left unoccupied. There was a cacophonous harmony of Arabic cries for the best jeans, sweetest melons, tastiest falafel. Some hawked fake Prada sunglasses and Nike cross-trainers. Fruit carts bandied up razor-thin streets past veiled women carrying babies, groceries for dinner. Resisting the urge to eat, I instead bought several exotic coloring books for my teacher friend's daughter, during which time I chatted with the merchant, who did not speak much English. I asked him how to get to Ramallah and if it was safe for someone like me—you know, someone tall.

"Of course, no problem, everyone is there," he gesticulated, scribbling something Arabic on a piece of paper and telling me to take it to Damascus Gate. From there he said people would know what to do. Though I didn't follow his instructions, I kept the piece of paper just in case. It was an exciting thought.

On the bus again, we headed back to the *kfar*. The trip was thrilling, if quick and disjointed. Players flaunted new souvenirs: pictures with camels, biblical ukuleles, a wooden flute, a camouflaged cowboy hat stenciled with YERUSHALAYIM, a handful of rosary beads. Several minutes later we were asleep, tired from the early wake-up call and excursion. And since Shabbat would be over with the setting sun, we'd be back on the field Sunday, the Israeli Monday and start of the week. But we had seen the Holy Land, if once and in frenetic spurts. We came, we saw, we joked, we bought. Not next year, as the traditional ending to the Passover seder intoned, but *this year* we were in Jerusalem. Amen.

8 Nokona Wreckin Crew

On the road from the *kfar* to Yarkon, the hills of Palestine were visible in the distance. We had traveled this route many times now, but I never knew we were approaching the West Bank as we headed to the field. Rothem said it was one of the slimmest parts of the country. He said Highway 5, which took us from the *kfar* to Baptist Village, led right there, was even called the Trans-Samaria Road because it dissected the northern part of the West Bank. But it was only for Israelis, especially the settlers. The Palestinians had a completely different set of roads for security reasons, as well as because their life patterns ran north-south whereas the Israelis' ran east-west.

After one of our games several days earlier I was speaking with a nice local family. We exchanged pleasantries, and they said how happy the IBL had made them. The family asked where I was from, and I returned the question. "We live in Samaria," the mother said. I looked at the husband, who was donning tzitzit and a yarmulke, growing curly *peyos*. Attached to the waist of his tweed trousers was a large, shiny silver pistol. He also had something furtively strapped to his ankle. I realized they were settlers, Israelis living over the Green Line in the occupied West Bank, which for them was simply the biblical land of Judea and Samaria, the greater Kingdom of Israel.[1] For others it was the land of Palestine, the land in which Muslim and Christian Arabs had lived for centuries. That whole cultural narrative thing. Any way you sliced it, I was steadfastly against the settler movement. *For* the state of Israel, to be sure, but *against* those Pharisees who believed a viable Palestinian state should not be allowed to exist. One could ruminate until Judgment Day on the politics of naming: Samaria or the West Bank, Israel or Palestine, Yerushalayim or Al Quds, Wall of Separation or security fence? But there was baseball to play.

As I exited the bus and prepared for the evening game, these incessant cogitations may have been the reason my first start in the IBL began so poorly. And to make matters worse, this was to be our first and only televised game of the season, under the lights at Yarkon Field.

Leading off, Reynaldo Cruz, Petach Tikva's stud six-three Dominican center fielder, laced a double to right center. Blazing around the bases, only the alacrity with which the ball smacked the fence prohibited Rey Rey from reaching third, before anyone knew what had happened. Great start, I thought. This one's on TV, and you give up a goat rope to start things off. Now you have to pitch from the stretch with a runner on and no outs.

"You're all right, mate. No worries!" shouted Wiggy, standing behind the plate.

Petach's number-two hitter was a lefty who did his job, grounding to second and moving Rey Rey over to third. Up next was the formidable Willie Bumphus, a soft-spoken former pro who

1. The Green Line is the common name for the Armistice Line, created at the end of the 1948 war, to demarcate the new state of Israel from its Arab neighbors.

journeyed to Israel after receiving a message from God in church one Sunday. Wiggy called for a fastball away, and that's right where it went. But it was no problem for Willie, who sent a blast deep to right. Jeff turned, sprinting immediately, and did not stop until his back was against the fence. His arm outstretched, he stuck his glove up high and came down with the ball just inches short of a home run. He threw it in quickly, but Rey Rey trotted home easily for the game's first run. I felt like everyone was beginning to look at me. The lights cast a magnified spotlight on the mound, on the guy who could not fool anybody and was getting banged around the yard. I had not even forced a single swing-and-miss.

Up next was Ryan Crotin. He was wearing eye black smudged down his face like a Rambo warrior. Underneath Petach's sleeveless jersey Ryan wore a skintight Under Armour T-shirt highlighting his massive arms. If he was not leading the league in home runs at this point, he was very close. With two outs, Wiggy and I started him off with a change, somewhat gutless but reasonable under the circumstances. I threw it weakly, bouncing it in the dirt for ball one. Our hand was forced. Everyone in the stadium knew what was coming.

CRACK!

The fastball screamed into the night on an upward trajectory. Our center fielder, Bryan Langbord, raced back toward the fence. He kept racing. Oh, fuck, I thought. Perhaps it was the evening humidity, for the ball drifted a moment too long, and Langbord came down with it just shy of the four hundred–foot sign in dead center. I walked off the mound slightly bruised, lucky to have given up only one run.

Needless to say, it was a slow start. My arm felt tight, and I did not have good stuff. The fastball was no mystery, and I had barely used the slider because I couldn't throw it consistently for strikes. After the first inning I began 1-0 a majority of the hitters. Working from behind in the count most of the game, it was a laborious outing. Yet my saving grace, for the second time, was the change. Thank goodness for the change. I could throw it for strikes, and, paradoxically, the tightness in my arm and low velocity on my fastball only augmented the pitch's effectiveness. I gave up one more run in the third, and we won 8–2. Our hitters were doing a great job. Jeff and Fish each had three knocks, and Brito dropped a BOMB in the fifth. Looking back on my line—seven K's, two walks, five hits—it did not seem nearly as bad as the rough first inning had augured. And going 2-4 at the plate was a cool bonus.

Afterward I was named the Nokona Player of the Game, which the league had invented for television to highlight the chief sponsor of equipment. Since baseball was not usually covered in Israel, announcers, broadcasters, everyone, learned on the job. This often made for good comedy. The two Israelis who had done play-by-play and color were now standing with me in front of the camera down the right-field line.

"Are you ready?" one asked.

"Sure."

"Okay, we're going to talk to the TV, and then we will ask you a question and you will speak."

"All right."

Each put his finger against his ear, straining to understand the Hebrew being fed through his earpiece. They nodded, "Yes, yes," and then looked up. "Okay! Welcome, ladies and gentlemen, to the first . . . to the . . ."

"Stop!" yelled the producer from behind the camera. "Do it again." They did it again, and again and again, finally getting it right.

"Shalom, welcome, ladies and gentleman, to the Nokona post-game wrap-up! I'm Jacob . . ."

". . . and I'm Devir . . ."

". . . and we're here with *Aron* Pribble, the Nokona Player of the Game."

"So, *Aron*, how did you feel?"

"To be honest, not great. Fortunately, my change-up was working and I could throw it for strikes. Plus I had a great defense behind me tonight—they really helped me out."

"Interesting. You seemed to get stronger as the game progressed, and in the last inning you even struck out the side."

"Well, I got off to a slow start. Their hitters, especially at the top of the order, are really tough. You have to give them credit. And like I said, our defense really did a great job tonight."

"Yes, it was a pitchers' duel up until the fifth when Stuart Breecko—"

"Stop! It's Brito. Do it again. Just take it from there."

"It was a pitchers' duel until the fifth when Stuart *Brito* hit a towering shot to left." As the announcers began recapping the highlights, I slid gently out of the picture. They wrapped up.

"Well, that's all from Yarkon Field where the Tel Aviv Lightning just beat the Petach Tikva Pioneers 8–2. *Lila tov*, everyone. Good night."

If that wasn't enough, Reynaldo was instructed to film a Nokona commercial, which proved difficult given his limited English. Fortunately, Jacob Levy, my Lightning teammate, was fluent in Spanish, and he helped Rey Rey through. The production team gave directions to Levy in English, who then translated them to Rey Rey in Spanish, who then mimicked the English he received from Levy. After several practice rounds, he was ready to go. Wearing a Nokona hat and batting gloves, bright-blue Nokona bat resting on his shoulder, he began, "My nane ees Reynaldo Cruz, from la Dominican Republic, an I part a la No-con-ah Wreckin Crew." He then swung the bat and smiled into the camera.

"Perfect!"

Rey Rey, though possessed of an intimidating athletic prowess, was quiet, almost gentle, off the field. In the first several weeks he had become a favorite of players and fans alike. Watching from the side, after Rey Rey smiled, so did I. Impressed with his ability to handle unique situations, I was also happy about the results of our game. Plus it was nice to be in second place, one game behind the undefeated Bet Shemesh Blue Sox. I began to feel my arm throb a bit, changing from simple tightness during the game, but brushed it aside. Even if I wanted to, there was no ice at the field. I would have had to cross the highway from the *kfar* to the gas station in order to grab a bag, ice my arm. Instead, we all went out to Bukowski's on Frishman Street in Tel Aviv, and the only icing I received came in the form of a cold beer.

9 Arm Trouble

The Israeli government agreed Sunday to restore full financial ties with the Palestinian Authority, now that President Mahmoud Abbas has decreed an emergency government with no members from Hamas. Israel will resume monthly transfers of taxes to the government as well as return, in installments, about $600 million withheld from the Palestinians since early 2006.

New York Times, July 2, 2007

How could my arm feel so bad so quickly? I woke up in the morning—slightly hung over—with a swollen wing that I could bend only slightly farther than ninety degrees. Pain shot sporadically down my arm throughout the night, but in my stupor I attributed it to the cardboard beds everyone was still getting used to. Staring at a falafel-size fluid sac surrounding my elbow, I tried to ascertain the cause of my current condition.

I felt fine after my first appearance, I thought. The last time I threw seven innings was in France a few summers ago; maybe the arm just wasn't up to it this time. I did have a little tendonitis while preparing in the off-season, I remembered, but that disappeared nearly a month before leaving.

Whatever the reason, something needed to be done. I stood up, gingerly put on a T-shirt, and held my arm in an imaginary sling as I walked past several peacocks to the common room, which was temporarily substituting for a training room (in fact, it would remain our training room for the entire season). Though at this point we did not have ice at the *kfar* or the field, we finally had trainers. Walking inside I encountered a squat, handsome version of Dr. Evil chatting with what appeared to be an aged swimsuit model.

"Hi, guys. How are you? I'm Aaron."

"*Aharon*, nice to meet you, man. My name is Tiger. I am the masseur," said the bald Ashkenazi with a sizable nose. Of course Tiger was the masseur, not his striking Sephardic partner.

"Hi, Aaron, I am Idi, the physiotherapist."

Both spoke proficient English, though Tiger's accent was more dramatic.

"So my arm isn't doing so hot. It's a little tender."

"Okay, let me see," said Idi. I laid on her portable training table, and she began to twist, turn, yank my arm. "How does that feel? That? Does this hurt?"

"No . . . no. Oooh, yep. No. Yeah-yeah-yeah." Though easy on the eyes, she was a rough therapist. Each time she collapsed and extended my arm I felt a smarting sting.

"You can only straighten your arm this far? This is not good. The joint is quite swollen. Look at this." With her finger she made a large indentation in the fluid sac on my elbow, which regained its form very slowly.

"All right. Now tell me when you feel pain," said Idi, poking and digging to the same effect.

"No, no. Yep—oooff!" It hurt like hell.

"Oh, don't be a sissy. I'm barely touching you." I heard Israelis were tough, but this was ridiculous. Tiger snickered from the other side of the room. Idi eventually focused her torture on the connection of the triceps tendon to the ulna, slightly below the funny bone and just to the side of the pronounced swelling. "You have tendonitis," she said. "Have you been icing and taking painkillers?"

"No. This just happened. Plus, we still don't have any ice. It's ridiculous."

"I know."

Tiger added, "They brought the machine in this morning, but it is not working. We are trying to fix it."

"Well, you need to be icing and taking something," Idi said. "You can get ice at the gas station across the street. And I recommend not throwing for a couple of days. You need to give your arm some rest."

"No, I've gotta throw. I pitch in less than a week, and I can't afford it."

"If you keep it up, you may just hurt yourself so you can't pitch at all. How about that? Try this: throw a few pitches, and if you start to feel pain, stop for a few days."

"That works," I said. I wasn't happy about the prospects of time off after just starting the season, but I knew Idi was right. On the other hand, what did Idi and Tiger know about baseball? Had they ever treated someone who played the sport? For that matter, did they know where shortstop was or the difference between a curve ball and a slider? But who cares? I countered. They were still qualified to treat the body. Even so, how were they equipped to assess and tend to the surfeit of sport-specific injuries that would inevitability arise? Dude, we don't even have ice, I thought. You gotta go with the flow.

After deciding on a course of action, Idi gave me some electric stimulation and ultrasound to warm up the elbow. I was frustrated and wished my thoughts were elsewhere. Fortunately, Tiger was feeling loquacious. He sat down next to me, and the three of us chatted about home and family, about contemporary issues. The previous day's *New York Times* had discussed troop buildups near the Israeli-Syrian border as possible indications of an impending war. I was captivated by the regional geopolitics while studying thousands of miles away, but the current relevance of potential war made it all the more engaging. Basically, I wanted a local's take.

"So, Tiger, do you think Israel will really go to war with Syria?"

"This is nothing new," he said flatly. "Here there is always conflict." Then he muttered something in Hebrew that made Idi laugh.

"What's that? What'd you say?"

Idi continued to treat my arm.

"Oh, nothing. In Hebrew we have an expression. We say, 'When you see the light at the end of the tunnel, it is only the train coming the other way.'"

I thought for a moment. The adage seemed a beautifully macabre encapsulation of the Israeli perspective.

"So there's no hope?"

"Hope? *Aharon*, you are such an American. Yes, we have hope, but it is always far away because there is always struggle. We live our lives every day. When one does not have high expectations, one is not easily disappointed."

Perhaps Tiger was right. Obsessing about peace and security in the long run only detracted from the intimacies of daily living. There would always be conflict. After all, it was much easier to move forward with one's life than with the peace process. Besides, a looming war with Syria paled in import compared to my sore arm. I was there to pitch, not save the world. That I would leave for teaching high school social studies.

I left the training room with a crippled elbow, a busy mind, and a growling stomach. I would have to eat something before testing out the arm. After another breakfast of cucumbers, pita, and cottage cheese I walked to the soccer field at the north end of the *kfar* to have a toss. My partner was teammate Jason Bonder, a stocky lefty who had just graduated from a small Pennsylvania college. Affable and caring, Bonder was, not surprisingly, strongly considering rabbinical school, though he would have second thoughts after our summer together in Israel.

"Thanks for throwing with me," I said. "I'm not sure how the wing feels, but we'll see."

"Oh, you're hurting a little? That's too bad. You threw really well last night."

"Thanks, man."

We were standing only a few feet apart. My heart beat rapidly as I sensed the weight of the next few minutes. I shook out my arm and then grabbed the ball and flipped it cautiously to Bonder. It didn't hurt much, but then again I had barely thrown the thing. I took several steps back, caught the ball. Again I flipped it lightly, and the pain slightly increased. I followed this same pattern twice more until realizing I needed to throw for real. Grabbing the ball, I smacked it in the pocket of my glove and took a deep breath. Upon release I suffered an explosion of pain. It felt like my elbow had punched me in the face. Hey, man, it said. I haven't done this shit in a while, so back off. If you want to hurt me, I'll hurt you. I'm drowning in disgusting fluid, and I can barely move. And you want me to help you throw again? Ha! Forget about it. How many times did we do that last night? Well over a hundred, I'm sure. You didn't even take care of me after; I sat there wallowing in discomfort. No ice bath, no drugs, just a little booze. At least you could have gotten me high so I didn't feel anything. *Don't* fucking do that again.

So I didn't. "Oooh-hoo-hoo, that's no good," I muttered, grimacing, looking down at the ground, trying to compose myself. I didn't want to blow up in front of Jason. Idi was right; I needed a little time off.

"Um, sorry, man. I don't think I can do it. I'm a little tight, and I should probably lay off."

"No problem, no problem. That really sucks. I hope you feel better," Jason said.

If there is any panacea for a sore arm, it is the ice-run-Aleve trifecta. In the following days I would begin to ice religiously and take painkillers 24/7. Thus became my life: ice-run-Aleve, ice-run-Aleve, and of course more treatment with Idi.

But with energy to burn I gave Bonder my glove and, disgruntled, burst out of the *kfar* on a noontime run. Being hurt was a shitty feeling, worse than sucking on the field. The physical pain was easier to overcome than the agony of not knowing if you'd miss your next start or the rest of the season. In the span of a week I had gone from not having good stuff in my first appearance to wondering whether I would even throw in my third.

Running through Ramat Hasharon, the town nearest the *kfar* just north of Tel Aviv, I wondered if this was the end of my short comeback. Maybe I would throw just twice after months of preparation and return home, tail between my legs. I hoped I wouldn't be the first player cut from the inaugural season of the Israel Baseball League, a dubious honor indeed. My first and only significant arm injury was during my second season of independent ball in Texas. In my first start of the year I threw a third-inning slider and felt a bite deep inside my elbow. That was a strained forearm; this was worse.

Forget about me. What was the Lightning going to do? Like every other team we had eight pitchers for six games a week, even if we were playing only seven innings. A professional squad with a comparable schedule would carry ten to twelve arms, at least two more than we had, assuming no one got hurt. It's true that fewer guys made economic sense from the league's perspective, but a deficient product was less likely to sell. It would also be harder to bring in fresh players from half a world away, though this did not occur to me when considering the prospects of getting released.

While jogging through quaint neighborhoods in the midday heat, these ruminations were cathartic, if irrational. A little self-pity was okay, provided one was focused in the end. The point was, it sucked to be hurt. This summer's ride had barely left the ground, and already it appeared to be stalling. I just wanted to play, good results or bad. What's worse, for all my kvetching I had no way of knowing my injury would pale in comparison to that sustained by Rey Rey several days later.

10 Fun and Games

THEY SAY IT'S ALL FUN AND GAMES UNTIL SOMEONE gets hurt. Thus far the lack of organization had simply been something to gripe about, but the somber reality of Rey Rey lying in a hospital bed with a brain aneurysm transformed our protests to anger.

Since Opening Day we had been pleading with the league to provide a minimum level of equipment, infrastructure, and protection. Sleeping three players to a broom closet and sending teams to games on the same bus left much to be desired, but they did not interfere with our safety. Perhaps the most dangerous thing about baseball is the condition of the field: a shoddy infield surface creates bad hops and loose dirt around the bases, a recipe for torn hamstrings and twisted ankles. Both had occurred in abundance at Kibbutz Gezer, the recently converted softball field on which IBL games were now being played. This was in addition to the rusty wrought iron protruding from the outfield fence and the light pole in the middle of right field. Although these were serious concerns, it would be an incorrectly performed warmup that led to our first casualty.

Most pregames proceed as follows: home-team stretch and batting practice (BP), visitor stretch and batting practice, home-team infield-outfield, visitor infield-outfield, first pitch, anthem, play ball. Anyone familiar with the game is aware of the basic rhythm of an infield-outfield. And most picture batting practice as a jocular home run derby, though the reality is more complex. A BP pitcher, often a coach, stands behind an L screen halfway to home, throwing as many strikes as possible. Three to five hitters at a time surround the batting cage, also referred to as a turtle shell because any ball not hit toward fair territory will be stopped by the convex screen around and above the hitter. In rotating sequences of five to seven swings hitters work on bunts, hit and runs, going to the opposite field. And, yes, the final round is usually swing away, code for let's-see-how-far-you-can-hit-it.

In addition, another several players are running the bases during this time. When the batter executes a hit and run, for example, the runner on first sprints to second, eventually running wide around third so as not to get hit by a line drive. Between each swing a player standing adjacent to the batting cage hits grounders to the infielders, who throw them to first, where another player is standing behind another large screen. Any and all balls hit to the outfield are thrown in to the bucket, located just behind second base. There, a disgruntled pitcher waits for a full load of balls, then runs them in to the pitcher's mound, dodging base runners, infielder ground balls, and lasers from home plate. Since the pitcher on bucket duty is standing with his back to home, there is another screen in front of him as well. With as many as five balls in flight at a time, one must be constantly alert during this symphonic pregame ritual.

This is how most batting practices are supposed to operate. Under the safest of conditions the potential for injury is high. Add to it an inferior playing surface and the risk increases. Subtract all screens save for the pitcher's L and it becomes treacherous, bordering on the insane. Welcome to the IBL.

This sunny morning the heat was becoming unbearable. Visiting Petach Tikva was lounging in and out of their dugout, waiting for Modi'in to complete its batting practice. Some of the guys were under the dugout tent, trying to keep cool. Others were putting on their uniforms, chewing the fat in the thin area between the dugout and the field. Paulino, Modi'in's leadoff hitter, had just taken his first bunt and hit and run. He then hit a laser, foul, which under normal circumstances would have hit the left side of the turtle shell and landed innocuously in the dirt.

CRACK! . . . CRACK!

Without such a shell, however, the unimpeded line drive struck Reynaldo Cruz, standing fewer than twenty feet from home, in the back of the head. The entire stadium fell quiet as Rey Rey lay twitching in the grass. Scotty Cantor said the sound of the baseball hitting Rey Rey's head was just as loud as the sound of the ball off Paulino's bat. It rolled all the way to the pitcher's mound. After an extended moment of unconsciousness Rey Rey eventually came to. He remembered his name but not where he was. Some of the players put an ice pack under his neck (ice was now provided at games), but this was about all they could do. An agonizing thirty minutes later the ambulance arrived, and the paramedics put Rey Rey in a neck brace, placed him on a stretcher, and drove him away.

Modi'in beat Petach Tikva handily, but the game was played under a cloud of anger and sorrow. Imperfect living conditions were par for the course in Minor League Baseball. They were to be expected and, I would argue, embraced. But patently unsafe conditions were unacceptable.

This day was a tipping point for the players, as well as the league. Rey Rey was lying in a hospital bed, uniform still on, far from his teammates and even farther from his Dominican home. Incredibly, he had suffered only a mild brain aneurysm and would remain in the hospital for several weeks. But he would never play baseball again.

Back at the *kfar*, grumbling and irritation turned to incensed criticism. Reynaldo's tragedy had coalesced players from all teams into a closer, more conscious fraternity. It wasn't enough that ambulances would be at games from then on. It shouldn't have taken sore arms to necessitate providing ice, or the end of a career to ensure proper safety precautions. Communication, though slightly improved, was still abysmal. What had seemed tolerable was no longer so. And when our first paychecks had still not arrived several days later, the IBL nearly ground to a halt.

11 *Huelga! Huelga!*

I HAD JUST SAT DOWN WITH JEFF, LEVY, AND FISH to a lunch of hummus and schnitzel when Brito approached, asking something about money. I told him the checks were here and that he could pick his up from Dan Saltzman in the library. Pulling out my check, I showed it to him. His usual cubbish demeanor turned to that of an angered bear, and he launched into an English-Spanish linguistic explosion. He was pacing back and forth, waving his large paw and pointing in various directions.

"Whoa, what happened, dude? What's going on?"

"Preebo. Dees guys, man. Dey . . . no money, man. Where dee fucking money, man?!" After a valiant attempt in English Brito jumped back into his mother tongue, that cut and mumbled brand of Spanish so indicative of the Dominican.

"*Mira, es solamente dos cientos cincuenta dolares—no quinientos.*" He pointed out that the check was for only $250 instead of $500, which I had overlooked.

"Oh, yeah. What the hell?" I said, looking nonplussed at the others.

"Thees es bullshit!" Brito proclaimed.

He was getting ever more impassioned. Brito began rattling off invectives in Spanish to his buddies sitting around us, starting a minor brush fire that spread throughout the caf like a blaze. After some hubbub about what they were going to do, Juan Feliciano, the Blue Sox's ace pitcher, stood up and valiantly announced, "Us Dominicans, we no play today!" With that they all stomped out, chanting, "*HUELGA! HUELGA! HUELGA!*" (Strike! Strike! Strike!). The only Dominican left was Franco, our shortstop, who calmly sat and finished his meal like he had been through this sort of thing a thousand times. When done he slowly walked out and met up with the others.

After the Dominican evacuation, Jeff, Levy, Fish, and I remained at the table, trying to make sense of the situation. We weren't sure why the checks, which came late to begin with, were for only half the purported amount.

Fish said, "Yo, if these guys strike, we need to make a decision about what we're gonna do."

"I wanna do what's right," said Levy. "But I'm not sure what that is."

"Well, our bus leaves in ninety minutes, so we'd better figure it out."

During the conversation Jeff wore a troubled expression, finally managing to say, "I'm just here to play ball." He was having a noticeably difficult time reconciling baseball and politics. I personally agreed with Levy, not a common occurrence given his arch-conservative beliefs. If there was a legit beef we would support it, but we were also sensitive to the financial difficulties of this nascent league in the middle of the desert.

Just then the young official, Andrew, walked in.

"This is fucked up, man," Fish said. "What the hell is going on? The Dominicans are about to strike." This would have sent others into a nervous blitz, but Andrew was competent at squelching similar fires and had already done so myriad times in the opening weeks of the season. He simply sighed, shrugged his shoulders, and gave us an exasperated smirk.

"All right, fellas, I'll see what I can do." Andrew made several calls, including one to the commissioner, Dan Kurtzer. When he got off the phone Andrew spouted that he *told* them this shit would happen, but they hadn't listened. I could have speculated about who "they" were, but it seemed fruitless. At this point, no one knew where the Dominicans were or what they were up to.

After washing down the schnitzel with some cabbage and a beet salad, we strode toward the dorms, past a family of peacocks, to pick up our clothes strewn as usual six-ways-from-Sunday on the decrepit basketball court. At least they were doing our laundry. Cresting a gentle slope outside the caf we noticed a large gathering of players, far too many to be simultaneously scavenging for socks and sliding shorts. The Dominicans were there, heated. Alan, the lawyer and Bet Shemesh outfielder, attempted to get everyone's attention. He held up a contract, and the crowd of players drew closer.

"Hey, guys, gather 'round. I've read this, and there's some stuff you should know."

Alan said that if we decided to strike we would be in breach of our contract, so the league would not have to pay the remainder of our salary, or for our flights home. Thus, we needed to speak with one voice, since the stakes were high. As Alan finished, the momentarily quiet crowd burst into a cacophony of questions and comments. Not a good sign for worker solidarity. Some countered that the league would not make good on its contractual threats, since no players meant no IBL and numerous people had invested too much money for this thing to end now. They said players therefore held the power and if we didn't get paid in full, we shouldn't play. Others were of the Jeff Hastings mold: they just wanted to play ball. The Dominicans were steadfastly against playing since Julio, the brother of Vladimir Guerrero, perennial Anaheim Angels All-Star, would simply write a check and fly them all home. At this point there was clearly no "one voice," as Alan had implored.

A little while later Commissioner Kurtzer rolled in. I had tremendous respect for him. Formerly a U.S. ambassador to Israel, he was a key player in Israeli-Palestinian negotiations from 2001 to 2005. Now a professor at Princeton, he took the summer off to be the IBL's first *honorary* commissioner—not to solve problems and squelch fires. He probably envisioned a lot of ceremonial ribbon cutting and first-pitch throwing, rather than returning to the Middle East for an entirely different round of negotiations.

He appeared frustrated upon arrival. Everyone was huddled together with our newly appointed labor lawyer, Alan, at the head of the group. The commissioner stood in the center of the basketball court, surrounded by laundry and a swarm of grouchy players. I was standing toward the back, as I held Commissioner Kurtzer in high regard and was uncomfortable with the prospect of a confrontational exchange (plus it was unbearably hot every-where except for a shady patch under the trees).

"Before we start, I want to be very clear. I will not have this conversation under threat of a strike," Kurtzer opened.

Alan countered, "Well, the league is in breach of contract since we were not paid, in full, on the appropriate date." He rattled on, and some of the Dominicans became visibly nervous. They looked unsure if Alan was to be trusted with their livelihood, and they clearly did not understand all that was said.

"Hey, man, no *money*, no play," interjected Feliciano. The Dominicans started to walk off.

"Whoa, whoa, whoa," we said collectively. They thought about it, returned. One of the bilingual players from Florida, Johnny Lopez, came to the front to translate so all could understand. I thought he did a good job given the circumstances, though later the Dominicans would feel that Johnny had sold out, siding with the league and not properly having their backs.

After passionate negotiations in two languages an accord was reached. The conversation became intense but never threatening, a relief considering it was 120 against 1. At times players interjected with useless comments like, "Yeah, right. When has this league done *anything* right?" but there was for the most part a reasonable amount of give-and-take. It was finally agreed, in fact promised, that we would receive the second half of our money the following week. The commissioner effectively argued that the first half of the check should be viewed as a good-faith down payment on the outstanding balance. If our money did not arrive, Alan and Johnny made clear that all options remained on the table.

Though we would receive the latter part of our checks as promised, many players would be denied their fourth and final payment at the end of the summer. My final check, for example, bounced twice within my first month home. A supplementary check mailed a year later would also bounce, resulting in the loss of a quarter of my total salary, never to be recompensed. This was okay considering the lavish incomes of teachers, but it was unacceptable for those athletes, such as the Dominicans, who needed the money to feed their families. Perhaps we should have gone on strike after all.

Later that night I ran into Andrew. "Shit, man, today was crazy. The IBL almost *ended*," he confided. It seemed the entire ordeal sprang from a profound lack of communication, portending similar events in the months to come. If everyone was told we would not be receiving the full amount during our leaguewide meeting one day prior, the entire episode could have been averted. In addition, during the impromptu collective-bargaining summit, some thought the commissioner should have employed more tact. Nevertheless, I sympathized with his having to heed stupid comments by untoward players, in a difficult, thankless position.

He was not responsible for the league's insolvency, though none-theless in charge of player relations. To his credit he quelled the first major uprising within the league. So much for the glory of a diplomat. Perhaps peace rather than professional baseball was a more achievable goal in the Middle East.

No sooner had a temporary agreement been reached between labor and management than an additional problem occurred, this time concerning the method of payment. We were issued U.S. checks, and many players were discovering they could not be cashed in Israel. In yet another round of negotiations it was agreed we would be paid in shekels. But this did not sit well with the Dominicans. I was beginning to think they were somewhat insensitive to the exigencies of the IBL. That is, until I discov-ered why.

The next day, fresh with money to burn, Jeff and I were prepar-ing for a nice breakfast in Ramat Hasharon when we saw Brito walking up the road.

"*Oye, muchacho.* Come eat with us, man," I called to him from across the street.

Walking over he said, "Sorry. *No puedo.*"

Often the Dominicans were invited out, but they rarely came. Some interpreted this as a rebuff, an indication that they were too cool to hang.

"*Adonde vas*—where you going?"

"*La oficina de correos,*" he answered.

I began to inquire when it hit me like a ton of bricks. No wonder the Dominicans wanted neither shekels nor checks. No wonder they didn't go out with us in Tel Aviv. Brito was going to the post office . . . to mail his salary back home. I felt like a huge schmuck. Upon further inquiry, I discovered that many of the Latino players were their families' sole source of income. In addition to supporting mothers, fathers, sisters, and cousins, many had multiple kids of their own. Although two grand might not go very far in the States, it could be stretched a long way in the Dominican Republic. There I was, wanting play money for a memorable experience, while these guys had mouths to feed.

"Come on." He crossed the street wearing an immense boyish grin yet looking unsure of what to do. I reached into my wallet under the table. "Come eat with us," I repeated as he approached, slapping some shekels in his hand as subtly as possible. Evident in his deep, full eyes was a sentiment of appreciation. Feeling a bit of Jewish guilt, I thought about how lucky I was to play ball solely for the love of the game. Brito sat down, and we shared a glance of mutual recognition. But a glance is about the limit of schmaltz for ballplayers, so I said, "Just get me a couple knocks when we play Bet Shemesh tomorrow. I'm gonna need 'em." Bet Shemesh had emerged as the league front runner, and it was my first time competing against their formidable squad.

Brito chuckled. "Sheet, man. We get those guys."

"That's right," I replied, belying an already nervous stomach.

As we ate I thought about the near strike the previous day and the commissioner negotiating with a lawyer–left fielder. I thought about Johnny Lopez translating myriad demands and explanations. I thought about Brito's family back home receiving his money. I thought about my arm. And though I tried not to, most of all I thought about the Bet Shemesh Blue Sox.

12 The Mighty Black Sox

The Israeli government on Sunday gave its approval for the release of 250 Palestinian prisoners to bolster the administration of Mahmoud Abbas, the Palestinian president, an Israeli government spokesman said.

New York Times, July 8, 2007

How did I make it to the sixth inning giving up only one run to Bet Shemesh? Come to think of it, how was I pitching at all? Just seven days earlier I had woken up with the worst arm pain of my career, no exaggeration. Although the regime of ice-run-Aleve, and of course beaucoup treatment with Idi, had worked well, I was still not 100 percent. Maybe not even 85. I was thus forced to ask Skip for an additional two days off, making Crabb throw on four days' rest instead of five. The upside was I could throw a baseball again, sort of. The downside: another televised start at Yarkon; a lot of fans, reporters, and cameras; and an intense microscope. Adding to the hype, we were in second place, while the Blue Sox, managed by Jewish former Yankee and first-ever designated hitter Ron Blomberg, were currently an undefeated 8-0. The league front runner, Bet Shemesh was quickly becoming the Yankees of Israel. Their navy-blue pinstriped uniforms with an overlapping *Beit* and *Shin* logo—like the *N* and *Y* of the Yanks'—only added to the resemblance. That and they had a Jeter, A-Rod, and Giambi of their own.

Before the game, however, I observed a small detail that seemed to absolve them of their demigod status. In true IBL fashion, the Blue Sox's socks were, in fact, black. It seemed no one was beyond the sphere of ironic influence of the Israel Baseball League. The Blue Sox had black socks. They were human after all. They could be defeated.

The bottom of the sixth inning was a particularly crucial spot. Up 3–1 we needed a mere six outs for the win. The sun had just set, and crisscrossing twilight shadows gave way to artificial light from the poles above. As a starting pitcher there are times to relax a bit and times to really gear up, according to the ebb and flow of the game. This was not a time to relax. With the top of the order looming, the sixth inning would make or break the game. The Bet Shemesh fans seemed to sense the urgency of the situation as well. The Blue Sox's performance thus far in the season had expanded their fan base to a disproportionately large, and loud, level. During the entire game not more than a handful of people were rooting for Tel Aviv.

Although it was early evening, I had long since sweated through my cap. Every time I touched the brim, I had to wipe my hand against the left side of my pants in order to get the correct feel on the tips of my fingers. Not wet but not completely dry, either. Stepping up the mound under the lights, I secured my footing on the rubber: feet wider than a bowler's but closer than a cowboy's, right about shoulder-length apart and slightly bent.

All right, let's go. I released a quick breath and looked in for the sign. Shaking my left arm in order to keep it loose, I began to feel a throb in my elbow. It started talking, but I shut it up. "Just get me six more outs."

Behind the plate Wiggy put down an index finger and pointed toward his left knee, calling for an outside fastball to the left-handed leadoff hitter. Taking a small step back to begin my windup, I heard Wiggy say in his thick accent, "Come on, Prib, let's go."

Ball one. Strike one. The count was even. I threw a slider, and the lefty grounded out to Frankie at short.

Up next was Greg Raymundo, the Blue Sox's Derek Jeter. He was drafted twelve picks *in front* of Albert Pujols in the 1999 draft, playing infield for both the Royals and the Pirates, making it as high as triple A. Greg had also been responsible for their only run of the game, a one-out RBI double over the third base bag in the third inning. This guy could hit. He currently held a batting average over .500, a ridiculous stat in any league. Greg smacked a 2-1 fastball sharply to short, but Frankie scooped the grounder gracefully, flicking it to Brito at first. Two outs.

The third hitter, Jason Rees, was the Blue Sox's Alex Rodriguez. An Aussie surfer with frosted, spiked hair and silver chains, like A-Rod he was particularly popular with the female-fan demographic. Down two runs Rees could not tie the game with a single swing. But I did not want to give the Blue Sox's lineup any opportunity to get back in the game, especially with Johnny Lopez, the translator and bomb-dropping first baseman à la Jason Giambi, hitting cleanup. The last two at-bats Rees flew out to deep center, then lined out dangerously to second. Both times he hit fastballs early in the count, which indicated he was an aggressive hitter.

Knowing I had scant left in the tank, I hoped Rees would be equally aggressive this time. I threw him a change on the outer third of the plate, intending it to look like another first-pitch fastball. He pivoted, let his hands fly, took a huge hack. Out front, he hooked the third grounder of the inning to Franco at short, who gobbled it up and delivered it efficiently to first. Walking off the mound with a surge of adrenaline, I could feel the end of the game drawing near. Just three more outs. But I could also feel a throbbing in my arm.

In the top of the seventh we went down in order, one, two,

three. Fortunately, so did they. It was Bet Shemesh's first loss of the season and my second prime-time win, putting me at 3-0 overall. Okay, okay, you'll get your painkillers when we get home, I told the voice. Considering how it felt a week earlier, this performance was unexpected. Beyond relieved, surprised, even stunned, I did not know if my stubborn elbow would allow me to throw a full seven innings, let alone pitch well. "Thanks, good buddy," I muttered schizophrenically.

Returning to the dugout after shaking hands with our team, I heard a voice behind me saying, "*Aron*, you are zee Player of zee Game. Congratulations."

"Oh . . . thanks."

Still in a daze, talking to my elbow, I felt myself being pulled down the first base line toward a TV crew, introduced to an attractive anchorwoman for Arutz Five Sports named Eleni. The light behind the camera shone brightly, and I tried not to squint. I thought about the interview the previous week and remembered some important advice I'd received watching *Bull Durham* at an early age: know your clichés.

"*Aron*, how did you feel tonight?"

"Pretty good." I didn't want to tell her about my aching elbow. "I just tried to throw strikes and keep the ball down. I had a great defense behind me. Frankie—I mean Franco—did a great job at short. He was like a black hole all game."

Suddenly I perked from my stupor. Something behind the camera had grabbed my attention, and I tried in vain to conceal a grin.

"Bet Shemesh was undefeated. Tonight you gave them their first loss."

With only six teams in the league, this was not the last time I would face the Blue Sox, so I tried to be as self-effacing as possible. There was nothing worse than giving a good team extra incentive to beat you. Plus, if I started laughing, they might think I was being disingenuous or showing them up. *Bull Durham*, I reminded myself, trying not to think of the figure darting back and forth behind the camera. "Hey, Bet Shemesh is a great team. They were undefeated for a reason. I was just lucky to throw strikes and let my defense do the work. We just gotta take it one game at a time. Lord willing, everything will work out." Maybe I'd gone too far with the last part.

"*Aron*, thank you."

"*Bevakasha*," I said, breaking into a large chuckle once finished. There was nothing particularly funny about Eleni's questions, but Wiggy had been prancing around behind the camera, pulling down his pants, giving me the finger, messing with me the entire time. Barely completing the interview before bursting into laughter, I wondered if *Bull Durham* had any advice for dealing with a bumbling Australian.

We loaded up, got on the bus to head back to the *kfar*. I grabbed a seat next to Crabb.

"Nice job, mate."

"Thanks, dude."

"So, your arm really hurt after all? I bet you just wanted another TV start. This league's only been filmed three times, and you've been on two of 'em. Why don't you spread the love a bit, you fuck." His ribbing was well placed.

"Nah, I think I'm gonna wait to throw until I'm *sure* we're on TV. I bet you're fine throwing on three days' rest."

"My arm's rubba, mate. No worries hea. Just make sure you get healthy. We picked up a game on Bet Shemesh tonight, but we're still trailing by one. I think it's gonna be a close season."

13 Shabbat Shalom

SEVERAL DAYS LATER, WHEN ROTHEM INVITED ME and Jeff to his mom's house for Friday dinner, I was excited and nervous. An item on my things-to-do-in-Israel checklist was having Shabbat with a local family. As an added bonus I would be sharing this experience with two nascent friends. Counterbalancing my zeal, however, was a measure of anxiety over the evening's pious ceremonies. The goyish Jeff had a free pass, but I claimed to be a Jew, sort of. Without a bar mitzvah, unless you counted the forced recitation of Torah in a Tel Aviv shul on Birthright two years prior, and short of a prayer or two from Hanukkah and Passover, my knowledge of Hebrew was next to nothing.[1] I hoped I would not expose my general lack of religious convention, though this was probably to be expected from a half-blood such as myself.

1. Funded by private donors as well as the state, Birthright sends young Jews to Israel for a free ten-day expedition, in hopes of strengthening the connection between the Holy Land and the Diaspora. It is an amazing trip.

On the ride over Jeff and I were beginning to salivate. The cafeteria food had taken a significant toll on our palates, and the thought of a home-cooked meal was orgasmic. For lunch and dinner on a daily basis it seemed as though we could not escape the dreaded schnitzel. Thin and dry, these breaded, fried, processed chicken patties were emerging as our nemesis rivaled only by the Blue Sox. Suffice it to say, we were ready for a change.

"Do you guys like schnitzel?" Rothem asked from behind the wheel. Jeff and I gave tense chuckles, unsure if he was serious.

"Um, yeah."

"My mom makes the best schnitzel around." There was an awkward silence. "You guys don't like schnitzel, do you?"

"Nah, nah . . . Yeah, it's good," Jeff and I fumbled. "It's just that it's like the only thing they serve at the caf so we kind of eat it a lot."

"Oh, *that* schnitzel," Rothem laughed. "That's not the real thing. That's like McDonald's schnitzel. You wait. This schnitzel is the best." Slowly, Jeff and I began to feel better about dinner.

"Where does your mom live?" Jeff asked.

"Jaffo." Dan explained that the town, pronounced "Yaffo," was predominantly Arab-Israeli and located just south of Tel Aviv, pre-dating the latter by many years. It was a bit poorer but overflowing with style and charm, much like San Francisco's Mission District. Jaffo was currently being revitalized, though this also included a degree of gentrification, hence Dan's mom's purchase of a newly constructed apartment in a cheap yet rising neighborhood. I noted as much to Dan, who replied sardonically, "Yes, we Israelis are taking over Arab land in Jaffo just like everywhere else."

Before reaching our destination, Dan stopped at one of the few liquor stores in the area because Jeff and I did not want to arrive at our first Shabbat empty-handed. As I exited the car Dan said, "Get a wine from Israel proper, but not the Golan. It's Occupied Territory, and we don't support that." I paused for a second and agreed. Though our beliefs regarding the conflict were quite similar, mine were academic, whereas his had been shaped by daily life. He had been in the army, driven tanks. The Golan was a place I had read about, once visited, and could locate on a map. For Dan it was a three-hour drive northeast of home. Whereas I might examine the conflict in graduate classes or discuss it with high school kids, Dan's knowledge, his understanding, was existential.

I thought about Birthright, rafting the hallowed River Jordan, over which Joshua led Israelites into the Promised Land, the site of Jesus's baptism, nourishing the Garden of Eden. Fed from Lebanese tributaries and Syrian springs, bordering the contested Golan Heights to the east, flowing into the Sea of Galilee, forming the Israeli-Palestinian border with Jordan to the south, ultimately completing its journey at the Dead Sea, the Jordan's water was a vital source of life, and conflict, in the Middle East. But back then, traveling through Israel with thirty young Jews, a guide, and an armed security guard, paddling down a stream diminished by damming, I was not thinking about the river's historical, religious, or political significance.

We arrived at our destination with a Flam cabernet from the Kinneret region, also known as the Sea of Galilee, where Jesus purportedly walked on water and Jews now turned it (and grapes) into wine. This particular section of Jaffo was the urban-planning equivalent of a geological subduction zone, one of the few places where large-scale, slow-moving change was evident. Hundred-year-old structures replete with traditional Islamic archways and geometric tapestry collided with half-finished modern apartment complexes.

"*Pop-pop-pop!*" Three loud shots rang out from just behind a large stone wall. Jeff and I jerked our heads down, anticipating a firefight.

"What the heck was that?!" Jeff exclaimed.

Dan muttered to himself in Hebrew, "Probably nothing."

We walked cautiously into a construction zone, through two

doors, down a secretive flight of stairs, and around a corner into a large protected courtyard. Just then two bright-green dots with tails of gray smoke sailed into the air.

"*Pop . . . pop!*"

Dan's irritated expression faded. Some kids were having a little fun with fireworks over the wall. He shook his head, smiled sarcastically, and said, "Fucking Arabs." We walked into the apartment complex and passed a couple headed the other direction. Dan exchanged pleasantries with them in Hebrew. Upon seeing the two Americans they grinned and said, "*Intifada*," referring to the ongoing fireworks display that sounded more like a gun battle.

"*Ken*," I replied with a chuckle as the couple walked past, showing off my vast knowledge of Hebrew.

"In-tee-fa-duh—what's that?" Jeff asked.

"Shaking off."

"What?"

"Tell you later," I said and gave him a shove, figuring he did not want to hear about the Palestinian uprisings in Gaza and the West Bank in the late 1980s and again at the turn of the century. Necessary or otherwise, Israeli occupation of these lands was controversial and had resulted in countless deaths on both sides.

We entered the small yet inviting apartment. Stone floors cool to bare feet gave way to a kitchen and living room sandwiched one on top of the other. We were introduced to Dan's mom, Ziva; brother, Asaf; and aunt, Shanik. Dan's cousin Orr, our backup right fielder known as Thor the Red Beard for his light skin and strawberry hair, was there too. Conversing with them, I felt immediately at home. After a necessarily quick tour of the apartment I found myself on the balcony with Dan's mom and aunt, leaning on the third-floor railing, looking into the dusk.

"It's beautiful here," I said.

"Thank you," replied his mom, smiling warmly. She spoke proficient English but seemed a bit shy about her accent. I was thinking of something to say when she pointed to the land just outside the courtyard.

"You see this?" She motioned with her hand. "This is all Arab. We are a settlement here in Jaffo," she said half-jokingly. Answering with a chuckle, I was uncertain of how to respond. Dan clearly did not support the settlements, but I was unsure about his mom.

Shortly thereafter food appeared on the table, and we were ready to eat. Unfortunately, my angst over the premeal rituals returned. I had flashes of challah bread, Elijah's cup, and havdalah candles. I seemed to remember the words "*Borei pri hagafen*" but couldn't remember what they meant. I started sweating (more than usual). It was a Shabbat meltdown. I'd be laughed at, disowned by my tribe. I was toast.

"So . . . if you guys do, like, prayers and stuff, I'm just gonna watch. I don't really know what I'm doing."

"Me too," Jeff added.

"Prayers?" Dan laughed at us. "We don't do any of that. I just come to eat." He sensed my trepidation and patted me on the shoulder. "You'll be fine."

Except for the heavenly garlic mashed potatoes and divine schnitzel, there was nothing religious about the meal. We began with a peppery cabbage slaw and a traditional Israeli salad of diced cucumbers, onions, and tomatoes. The schnitzel came next, and it did not disappoint. The lightly breaded, thick kosher chicken slices were succulent, tender. Jeff and I indulged like we had not had a home-cooked meal in weeks, which was true.

The conversation at dinner ping-ponged between Hebrew and English. We spoke about Israelis being crazy drivers, our first league games. Everyone was cognizant of keeping Jeff and me involved, but there was often lively dialogue in the mother tongue that I did not understand. In addition to chatting with Jeff during these moments, I reflected on Shabbat in general and this meal in particular. I thought the weekly creation of a space to slow down, to pause, to put the fast-paced life on hold, was imperative. It might be Friday night or Sunday afternoon; the important part was spending quality time with friends and family, whatever the religious or cultural pretense. And there was no pious rigmarole this night. We ate, we drank, we laughed. Some may not have called it a Shabbat at all. For me, it was a wonderful time.

At one point the conversation seemed to take a turn for the argumentative, but since it was in Hebrew my comprehension was limited to volume, inflection, and the occasional word or two. A fervent exchange such as this, I imagined, could only be about politics. Voices raised, hands flew up in exasperation, and homemade pickles were devoured like ammunition, but no one appeared angry. In fact, all seemed to be enjoying the tête-à-tête. Suddenly, the discussion turned quiet. Dan's mom leaned in close over the table, looked squarely at Jeff and me, and said, "Dan—he is a Palestinian!" referring to her son's leftward political views. His entire family began to laugh, and Dan looked slightly irritated. Just like on the balcony, I could not tell if his mom was serious. In any discussion about the conflict, sarcasm and sincerity were close friends.

As the meal wound down I could take only shallow breaths, a full stomach encroaching on my lungs' room for air. I dreamed of a couch to lie on, but along came desert: watermelon, cantaloupe, some strange fruit I did not recognize.

"What's that?" Jeff asked.

"Prickly pear," said Orr.

"We call it *sabra* in Hebrew," Dan's aunt interjected. She explained that this fruit was the informal name for Israelis, because they were prickly and tough on the outside from years of toil in the desert, yet remained sweet on the inside. I tried one. The fruit's flesh was sugary, though the seeds were pesky and difficult to get rid of. You could chew and swallow them, but they went down rough. You could spit them out, but with everyone watching this was a bit awkward. Sort of like the Israelis themselves.

After the meal everybody reclined lethargically in the living room, which was really the same space as the kitchen and dining area. A Mets-Cardinals game was rerunning on the muted TV, providing ambient background stimulation, the modern-day fireplace. Someone asked why baseball in Israel had not caught on before. Dan's aunt posited that Israelis were impatient and baseball was just too slow. She said they preferred the dynamic action of soccer and basketball. Dan said in fact there had been baseball in Israel for two decades, and Orr rebutted that even though he was correct, this was the first year it had arrived *professionally*. Dan's brother thought that it was a failure of management. The people who were first involved in the game here, he said, made it a backyard sport and nothing more. Dan then gave a threefold retort about Israelis watching but not really seeing the game, not knowing where to look for the action, and expecting a lot of "points." Everyone agreed that, whatever the reason, we all wanted it to succeed in the present.

When it was time to go we stood up and said our good-byes.

"Thank you very much. It was great," I said to Dan's mom, giving her a hug. Jeff did the same. Dan whispered to me that he was a bit chagrined about his family's dinner-table argument, especially his mom's ribbing. I replied that this actually made me feel more at home. Combine equal parts embarrassment and guilt, mixed with an abiding need to feed the planet, and you have any Jewish mother. I missed mine.

"You are welcome," his mom said. "I see you next week. We are having ravioli."

We did come the following week, as well as the next week and the week after. I did not know it at the time, but Shabbat in Jaffo would become as regular as my starting against the Blue Sox. Both were exciting, though the latter would get a bit old. And though our Shabbat dinner had come to an end, our Friday night was just getting started.

14 Sabras

THAT NIGHT WE MET UP WITH FISH, LEVY, AND THE rest of the guys. After some deliberation we decided to hit the hip, funky bars of southern Tel Aviv. And without expecting to, Fish and I met a couple of sabras of our own.

We stopped first at the Mish Mish on Lillenblum Street. It was a dimly lit two-story pub with hardwood everything, at once swanky and dilapidated. We grabbed a beer at the sparsely populated bar before heading upstairs to look around. A few of the tables were occupied with midsize groups who appeared uninviting, so we clustered on the railing overlooking the floor below. A few beers later we still clung to the railing, so to mix it up Fish, Jeff, and I made our way, once again, to the bar.

"Pribble, get in there."

"Huh? You guys need another beer or something?"

"No, get in *there*," said Fish and Jeff in unison. I turned around and nearly ran into her. I could see only her profile. The outline of her face was sleek, striking. Wavy black hair flowed behind her ear, down her neck, to the middle of her bronze back, covered in a turquoise spaghetti tee. She was tall and slender, her jeans hugging tightly the contours of her body. On her feet were fashionable black flats.

Butterflies erupted in my gut like I'd just been summoned from the bullpen. I froze. Fortunately, she did not notice, and I had a moment to collect myself. I had to do it.

"Excuse me," I said, leaning in over the bar just past her right shoulder.

She seemed momentarily caught off guard by the English and said curtly, "Oh, no problem." Prickly and unimpressed, she began to turn back toward her friend. I had to break through the tough exterior, but my window was rapidly shrinking.

"Just trying to, uh, grab a beer," I fumbled. She turned back around, nodded, and smiled politely. For a brief second I caught the gaze of her dark-green eyes. Pick it up, Pribble. "Sorry, I just . . . I'd speak Hebrew if I could . . . but I can't, so . . . ."

She interrupted my babbling. "Yes, you are American, right?"

"Yeah, from California."

"Why are you in Israel?"

"We're here playing baseball."

"Baseball—we do not have this sport in Israel."

"Yeah, I swear. Look." I turned to Fish and Jeff, who were pretending not to watch us intently.

"Guys, why are we here?" They answered, and she seemed convinced for the moment.

"I'm Aaron," I managed to say.

"Yael," she replied.

"Yael, nice to meet you. These are my friends Fish—I mean Nate—and Jeff."

"Hi. This is my friend Avi," replied Yael. Fish sidestepped behind Jeff and me to shake Avi's hand. They began chatting. Sometime later I was still talking with Yael, trying not to smile overtly, when

Jeff disappeared behind me to join Levy, Rothem, and the others who were now hovering directly behind us.

"We're gonna try the place up the street," someone said.

"*Yalla*—let's go."

After hopping in and out of a few more bars on Lillenblum, Yael and Avi miraculously alongside, we found ourselves at the Port in northern Tel Aviv. The Port was a beautiful mile-long stretch of wooden boardwalk lined with bars and eateries overlooking the Mediterranean. Dan had gone back home, and several of the guys ran into a particularly raucous lounge, so Yael, Avi, Fish, Jeff, and I sat down on two sofas at the outdoor Seabreeze Bar. Mist from the water made the couches slightly damp; occasionally whitewash from the sea landed at our feet. It was late into the night, and although many bars did not close until morning, ours was all but shut down. Nonetheless, we enjoyed the view, the ambience, the conversation. I learned that Yael was a Yemenite Jew living in Rosh Ha'ayin, where she studied architecture. Her friend Avi was in fashion.

Though we did not play the next day, we had risen early for our Friday-morning game. I could tell Jeff was fading, and I wondered about the girls. Observing the occasional yawn, it looked like everyone was a bit tired. "Okay, time to go, I think."

"Yes, it is very late," replied Yael. The look on Jeff's face said, "Thank goodness," though Fish was still in high gear.

We arrived at the *kfar* after finagling a ride from Yael and Avi. The three of us scrunched into the back of a compact red Peugeot was comical if nothing else. As Yael turned off the engine, Fish, Jeff, and I exchanged quick "What do we do?" glances. In a sign of our rapidly maturing friendship, no words were necessary. Since Jeff was married, he politely said good-bye and strode off to bed. With even math, Fish and I could entertain. Fortunately, the *kfar* was not short on mystery. We could go to the bunker, the horse stable, the soccer field, the library, or the peacock village or roam around the satellite university.

Instead, we settled on the petting zoo, literally. The first hint of light was beginning to peek over the palm trees and the barn. For Avi, Fish decidedly won a staring contest with an ostrich. I took Yael to see the llamas. And then I leaned in for a kiss.

She pulled away. "*Aron*, I am sorry."

I tried to brush it off. "Nah . . ."

"It's just that . . . I'm leaving for Germany tomorrow. My sister is there, and I am going to live with her. I think I should go."

I told her that she had my number, and in any case I'd love to hear from her. I had once played baseball in Germany, and maybe we could talk about the food, the architecture. But I knew it was for naught.

"I had a nice time, *Aron*. Good luck with your season. This *kfar* is a weird place."

"Thanks. Have a great time in Germany."

Nuzzling shoulder to shoulder, Yael and I walked back up the road to meet Fish and Avi, who were trying to pet baby rabbits through a fence. The four of us exchanged cheerful good-byes. Then the sabras went on their way, and Fish and I went back to our rooms, just short of witnessing our first sunrise in Israel.

15 Sportek

We hadn't played Bet Shemesh since the last time I pitched. My arm finally felt good enough to get back into the five-day rotation, but it meant I would be throwing against the Blue Sox once again. This time, however, we were playing at Sportek, the third and final field of the IBL—that is, if one felt comfortable calling Sportek a baseball field.

A week ago, several into our season, Sportek was sprawling grass in a vast community playground in northern Tel Aviv, just shy of the Port, where families and African immigrants played rec-league soccer. The fate of the baseball field was unclear until very late, when the newly elected mayor upheld the IBL's contract and decided not to give in to local soccer players, apoplectic that such a bizarre field was being built in *their* park. But due to typical bureaucratic rigmarole, work did not begin on the field until the season was well under way. The first actual game at Sportek was played just several days before this one. There were teams, emergency staff (a result of Rey Rey's injury), concessions, a PA, and, believe it or not, a few fans.

Construction having started so recently, it is not difficult to imagine the condition of the field. Wrought-iron poles were recently removed from the outfield, but a plastic utilities box was left dangerously below the grass in short center. It would remain for the entire season. The fence was some version of chain-link. But being Israeli, it was sharper, more rigid, and more dangerous than the American sort, just right for Hastings to get stuck in during our final game. Seriously. Sportek's dimensions were fairly odd as well. While left and center were close to regulation, the fence shortened precipitously in right, which was no more than 225 feet down the line. The genesis of this strange feature was a compromise reached between the league and the city, as a result of the rabid soccer players who could not believe such a foreign structure was encroaching on their sacred ground.

Believe it or not, the field's best feature was the mound, which Rothem and a few other Israeli players had spent two long days building themselves, with the sunburns to prove it. The infield, however, was the *worst* thing about the field. An insufficient amount of dirt was ordered, which meant that whatever rocky soil the bulldozers unearthed we would be fielding on, sliding into, and running around. As a direct result, over the course of the season one teammate would break his nose and another would pull from the dirt behind third a nail-infested two by four. This is to say nothing of the countless bad hops and errant bounces of which I have never in my life witnessed in greater abundance than at this field. As if it could not get any more preposterous, the backstop was still being built five minutes before our game.

In the top of the first my friend Jeff gave me a boost. Perhaps he sensed I needed a little something extra for my second straight match-up against Bet Shemesh. It was the best gift he could have possibly given me. Striding toward the plate to lead off the game, wearing an intimidating pair of jet-black Oakley's, his muscular figure and fierce scowl were more than enough to strike fear into the opponent. Jeff tapped both cleats with his bat and dug in to the box. We expected a first-pitch take and were caught off guard when he let loose a massive hack. "Aaaaaahh," we heard as he let out a large grunt while he swung. Our momentary surprise became adulation as he connected, sending the ball twenty feet over the left-field fence, a leadoff opposite-field blast. Thanks, Jeff.

In the third inning Bet Shemesh scored a run on a Greg Raymundo double, and in the fifth they manufactured a second when Levy missed a pop-up in left. As this brought the Blue Sox to within one run, I was displeased. I had the wild notion that even though we were close friends, the conservative Levy was trying to sabotage my potential victory simply because of our differing political views. I was going crazy. Just before these irrational thoughts got the best of me, Levy stepped up in the bottom of the same inning and smacked an RBI double, his second hit of the game and first runs batted in. This brought the score to 3–2. Thanks, Levy.

Throughout the game my stuff was okay. I threw the change and slider decently for strikes, spotting my fastball away. But for the life of me I could not hit the inside corner. In fact, both Blue Sox runs came on inside fastballs that got too much of the plate. I told Wigg to set up a ball or two farther inside so that if I missed, as I had been, it would cross the inside black instead of Main Street. Unfortunately, I was not having much success with this adjustment, either.

Making matters worse were the dugouts. There were no benches, only a few plastic chairs. Over them tarps were hung in tentlike fashion to block the sun, but this configuration also created a sort of wet sauna with no airflow. Moisture dripped from the plastic canvas roof. Though protected from direct sunlight, the dugout was also five to ten degrees hotter than simply standing outside in the occasional breeze. I sweat nearly as much under the tarps as on the mound.

In addition, I was laboring. Crabb would approach me after the game and ask, "How'd you feel, mate?" which was baseball code for, "You didn't look so good." Even though my arm had been getting better, it didn't feel great. In a typical game, my hat and undershirt soaked through completely. Today at Sportek, when my jersey and pants also became soggy, I knew I was sweating more than usual (since the field had barely been constructed in time for the game, I did not even think of asking for a rosin bag). It felt like I was wearing a life preserver, like the difference between running on the street and running in the sand: both required the same general motion, but one entailed significantly more effort. I was enervated, laboring, toiling, working much harder than typically necessary.

Going into the last inning the score was 4–2. Fish knocked in Frankie for a little extra cushion, but two runs are not much when you're running on empty. Standing on the mound just behind the rubber, I twirled the baseball in my left hand, looking for its highest seams. I found them, placed the ball in my glove, tucked the glove in my armpit, tugged on my hat, wiped the moisture from my fingertips on my damp left hip, wiggled my left elbow, bent slightly forward, and looked in for the sign. It was a particularly big moment. But this routine I repeated pitch after pitch, countless times a game.

I K'd the first hitter on a fastball away, a big at bat. Two outs to go. Next up was Mike "Sugar" Lyons. As he was an aggressive hitter, I managed to throw a first-pitch change for a strike, which he grounded slowly to Franco at short. Money, I thought, and turned my back. Two outs. Let's go for the th—

"Safe!"

I whirled around to see the first-base umpire crouched with his arms spread wide. Frankie had taken his time getting to the ball through the minefield at short, and Sugar Lyons could run like a gazelle. Shit. One out with a runner on. One swing could tie the game.

They pinch-hit for the eighth hitter and brought in a tall, athletic-looking righty I didn't recognize. As he was loosening up in the on-deck circle I noticed he had a long swing. Wiggy noticed the same. I stepped on the rubber and came set in the stretch, paying close attention to Sugar Lyons at first but barley noticing Wiggy's sign, both of us aware we were going to bust the hitter in. I also knew, however, that I had been unsuccessful throwing inside the entire game, which had led to both runs for the Blue Sox. It came as no surprise, then, that this fastball would also end up right down the heart of the plate. It met the hitter's long swing perfectly, rocketed to short. My initial fright as the ball left the bat turned to excitement when I realized it was a tailor-made double play. Frankie did a great job fielding the ball but was just a hair late shoveling it to our second baseman, Sammy, who double-clutched and was tardy throwing to Brito. Though we got Sugar Lyons at second, the hitter was safe at first.

Assuming the outcome of the double play, I thought the game was over and had to quickly refocus, which took a little extra work since I had nothing left in the tank. I was overflowing with emotion, trying to harness the energy, keep it under control, pissed that the double play wasn't turned. Usually, I kept that stuff to myself, since it's terrible baseball etiquette to so much as hint at showing up a teammate. But my emotions bubbled over. I looked back up the middle at Frankie and Sam, said truculently, "LET'S FUCKING GO! SHIT!" staring at them for a moment longer. I was pissed. Focus, Aaron. Okay, number nine's up, I thought. Two outs. You gotta get this guy 'cause if you don't, it's top of the order with two guys on.

I fell behind the ninth hitter 2-0. Two balls away from walking him and bringing up the leadoff hitter. Stepping off the mound, I mumbled a few epithets at myself for encouragement, trying to muster the strength for one more strike. I let loose a fastball right down the middle. It was grounded to Fish at third who flipped it to first to end the game. I took a deep, angry breath and walked up to shake Wiggy's hand. As I was still spewing under my breath, we turned around to high-five the rest of the team. This one had taken some work.

During Skip's postgame talk I settled down. The adrenaline rush faded, and I was thinking more clearly. Though satisfied with the win, especially since it was only the Blue Sox's second loss of the season, a sense of embarrassment crept in. What an asshole, I thought to myself. Those guys are doing their best, just like you. You're gonna suck someday (sooner than I imagined), and you don't want anyone getting on *your* case. You'd better make up for it.

When Skip finished talking I stood in front of the group. "Frankie, Sammy, I owe you guys an apology. You were lights out all game, and I shouldn't have shown you up like that. I'm sorry. It won't happen again."

"It's cool, dawg," Sammy said.

Frankie was characteristically mellow. He was lying on the grass with a dip in.

"*Ningun problema.* Es cool, man." It felt good owning up to my gaffe. I wished I could be cool as a cucumber, like Frankie, but I was straining to finish the game. It took everything I had, which was not much to begin with. If that included some bad language and a frenzied approach, so be it. At least we got it done. Baseball is about knowing where to get yourself mentally in order to have the best chance of success. Today it meant being a little crazy. Next time it would be staying calm during a near brawl.

Either way, the competitive juices hadn't flown like that in a while—certainly not in the classroom. The metamorphosis was complete: So long, Mr. Pribble. Hello, Prib. At that moment I was a ballplayer, the teacher buried somewhere beneath the cussing and the cockiness. A good thing, too, as I would need all the confidence I could muster after the trouble Frankie would give me later that night for my performance on the field.

16 *Para Bailar La Bomba*

Israel has agreed for the first time to remove 178 Fatah-affiliated militiamen in the West Bank from its wanted list, government officials said Sunday. It has also given extraordinary permission for several exiled Palestine Liberation Organization officials to attend a meeting of the group's Central Council this week in Ramallah, in the Israeli-controlled West Bank.

New York Times, July 15, 2007

BY THE TIME WE FINISHED EATING A DINNER OF schnitzel and hummus in the caf, we were the last ones present except for a few Dominicans chatting in a corner. We wanted to go out after the game, but we also wanted to hang with Frankie and Brito.

"*Oye*, Brito, Frankie, *que pasa?*" Levy called. They threw us a head nod from across the room.

"Let's get them to come out with us," Fish said.

"Yeah," I added.

Jeff was too busy drenching his chicken in ketchup to notice.

We walked over to their group and sat down at an adjacent table.

"*Que hacen anoche?*" Levy asked.

"*Vamos a La Bomba*," Frankie announced.

They were gonna go dancing? I didn't understand. "Where at?" I asked stupidly. Frankie looked confused and then pointed across the highway.

"*La Bomba.*"

"That's their name for the gas station," Levy informed us. We knew the Dominicans often went across the street to hang out, much like others went into Tel Aviv. So instead of another night on the town the four of us, along with a handful of Dominicans and some wandering peacocks, left the caf for *La Bomba*.

In order to get there one was supposed to exit the guard shack and walk down the street, up across the overpass, and then back up the road to the gas station. It was a giant U, much slower than simply darting across the highway, which we did regularly. The sight of us dashing past cars reminded me of those road signs in southern California, except that instead of a family crossing the highway it was an entourage of ballplayers.

La Bomba was a gas station, convenience store, and deli rolled into one. In addition to fuel it served sandwiches, pizza, groceries, appliances, and liquor. We grabbed a bag of warm assorted nuts and a smattering of tallboys and sat to the side on a large dilapidated retaining wall, some finding chairs to form a circle. At first there was a lot of English spoken among the Americans, Spanish among the Dominicans. It wasn't awkward but not completely natural, either.

Sensing a need to break the ice, Frankie stood up and quieted us down. "Sh-sh-sh," he said, palms flapping toward the ground. In the middle of the circle Frankie approached an imaginary home plate. It appeared as if we were getting ready to play some form of charades. Pretending to put on sunglasses, he puffed up his chest, tapped his cleats with his bat, and dug in to the batter's box. He took a huge swing. "Aaaaaahh," he said, letting out a massive grunt, running around the ring of guys substituting for a base path, ending up back inside the circle. Everyone looked at Hastings, whose face was flushed red, and we burst into laughter.

"No, this is how you do it." Jeff stood up and replayed his own grunt and home run, and we all cheered.

"Okay, okay, okay." Frankie quieted us down again for another round of charades. I got nervous. This time he walked up an imaginary mound, looking in for the sign. Nodding, he threw a pitch and spun around as it shot past him up the middle. Then he scampered back to the edge of the circle, fielded the ground ball, flipped it to second, turned around to receive his own throw, and tossed it to first for the double play. He was like Bugs Bunny in those old cartoons, playing each position. With Frankie moving uncharacteristically quickly, Fish and Brito were already beginning to chuckle. Frankie then shuttled over near first and yelled, "Safe!" after which he ran back to the mound. As the pitcher again, Frankie jumped up and down, shook his head, and threw an imaginary mitt to the ground. He walked back toward second and began to scream at two imaginary infielders. It was obvious Frankie was mocking my blowup in the last inning of our game, and I received several minutes of pointed yet good-natured ribbing. Frankie came over and slapped me five, and I gave him a friendly shove.

"Hey, at least we got the win," I said. "Whatever it takes."

"Yep, that's right," Jeff added. "A grunt or two never hurt either."

Things loosened up, and we were having a good time, conversing as freely as possible given the partial language barrier. We learned that Frankie had two kids, a little boy and a girl, while Brito had an eight-year-old daughter. Jeff told them he had a four-year-old son, Jayden. The three fathers bonded at once. Jeff and Brito even exchanged wallet-size photos. As faces lit up, talking about kids, the difficulty of leaving their families was evident. For Frankie and Brito it was expected, since baseball was their livelihood. For Jeff this was a summer of choice, one more under the sun before returning to a job, a wife, a kid, a mortgage, the end of a career. Whatever the reason, it was tough being away from their young families.

Throughout the evening various people joined the group. First it was the Australians: Wiggy, Crabb, and Jason Rees. Wiggy had just gotten his long blond surfer hair braided into cornrows, like Frankie. It was a terrible look, and we were sure to let him know. Next several other Dominicans came, including Feliciano, who had emerged as the league's best pitcher. He had not lost, having relinquished only a smattering of runs, which was to be expected since he played the previous year for the Hiroshima Carp in the Major Leagues of Japan. I'm not sure why he left.

At its zenith the group swelled to nearly thirty, which may have been why the cops came. Since drinking in public is not a big deal in Israel, the fuzz settled on ordering us from one side of the gas station to the other. They said there were reports of people smoking, that it was dangerous to be lighting fire directly on top of fuel tanks. Whatever. We suspected the true reason for the cops' appearance was the nervous night manager, understandably tense about a mass of foreigners cavorting on his property. For the most part everyone was respectable, though chairs may have been surreptitiously commandeered from the café and players could have been more environmentally conscious. Guys were throwing their tallboys over the wall. Throughout the night I sneaked back to collect the cans and recycle them, not so much because I feared the night manager's wrath but because my northern California sensibilities could take only so much abuse of Mother Earth.

"Pribble, what are you doing?"

"Oh, just taking a piss."

"Then why do you have all those cans in your hand? What are you—picking up trash?"

"It's nothing. Never mind."

While we talked late into the evening it seemed the Dominicans spoke of just two things: ladies and baseball. I feared for the occasional group of women who rambled into the gas station for fuel and snacks, as no one was beyond their penetrating gaze.

During discussion of the Dominicans' ostensibly two-tracked minds, Levy was reminded of a recent encounter. "Pribble, Fish, listen to this," he said, barely able to contain his laughter long enough to tell the story. "The other day I went into Brito's room to hang out with those guys. I walked in and saw them all hunched over a laptop, staring at the screen with crazy focus. They were elbowing each other and giggling. Of course I thought it was porn, and I hesitated walking behind the screen. But when I did I saw they were watching *cartoons*, I think *Tom and Jerry*. It was hilarious." Maybe this was an exception to the rule.

That they referred to each other by alter–baseball ego nicknames, however, was certainly not an exception. We discovered that Frankie was *El Ave Negro*, the Black Bird, because he swooped on ground balls with such grace and acumen. This was also, we later discovered, because of his particularly dark complexion. Brito was called *Pupo*, though I never figured out why. But without a doubt, the finest of all nicknames belonged to Netanya's shortstop, Hector De Los Santos. In the Minors he became known as *Matacaballo*, Horsekiller, for the way he slaughtered opposing teams' ace pitchers, or horses. He was also a remarkable fielder. During one game at Sportek, for example, Matacaballo jumped for a grounder that bounced over his head, barehanded the ball, and threw to first, all while still in the air. What a stud, pun intended.

In addition to this valuable cultural information, we learned an important lesson that night: to Dominicans, age is much more than a number. Fortunately, Wiggy made this mistake for all to see.

"Oy, Frankie," he said. "How old are ya, mate? You look like you've been playing this game foreva." I think he intended the comment as a compliment, but it came out quite the opposite. Frankie's face turned serious, and all the Dominicans became quiet.

"Me, I seventeen, man," he said sarcastically, and everyone laughed. Frankie nimbly ducked the question, but the moment was more telling than it seemed at first blush. When one's career was obsessed with youth, old age could be a death knell. Though

Frankie's IBL baseball card said twenty and Brito's nineteen, they were both clearly in their thirties. When I asked Frankie later in the season, because I couldn't resist, he said he was twenty-nine, the same answer I received from Brito. It seemed no one ever got any older. Thus, we uncovered an unwritten rule of professional baseball, Rule 29: never ask a Dominican his age. It is not difficult to understand why.

We filled the early hours of morning in this manner, telling stories, giving each other trouble, imbibing, getting to know those with whom, up to this point, we had not spent much time. Dominicans, Americans, and Australians, Lightning, Tigers, and Blue Sox, it brought us all closer together. This was the first of many nights we would spend at *La Bomba*. It became our plaza, our town square, our coffee shop. We commiserated there after losses, rejoiced after big wins. We blew off steam when needed and learned about other people and different places, intentionally or otherwise. In true IBL fashion it was not surprising our central refuge would be a crumbling retaining wall outside a gas station along a highway, paralleling a *kfar*.

17 The Love Doctor

SERIOUSLY AGAIN — THREE GAMES IN A ROW? DID I have anything else to throw at these guys? This act was *tired*. Conventional wisdom says the more times a batter faces a pitcher, the more advantage the batter gains. And I certainly wasn't about to learn a knuckle ball. I had three pitches, only two of which seemed to work in any one outing. The Blue Sox had the league's best record, most home runs, highest batting average. But like the ironic discovery of their black socks before my first outing, I had gathered another piece of humanizing intelligence: though *Bet Shemesh* meant House of the Sun, *Bet "Shemoosh"* meant House of the Toilet. From now on the mighty Blue Sox would be known as Bet Shemoosh, the Outhouses, the Toilets, the Lavatories, or some other scatological derivation thereof.

This being another Friday, games began at ten in order to end prior to the beginning of Shabbat at sunset, which meant most everyone arrived at the field in a fog. On the bus players were as grumpy as they were sleepy; there was no difficulty smelling who went out the night before. Furthermore, it was cruel waking at seven one day a week when the other five days we rose by noon in order to be at the yard around three. But that was the IBL.

I was getting loose in the bullpen when our team took the field, anticipating a start to the game. Perhaps I was dreaming. Still about six minutes from being warm, I glanced at my watch, surely not behind schedule. It was 9:50. Grouchy from the morning rise, fairly nervous facing Bet Shemoosh for the third time in a little more than two weeks, I hurled several tasty curse words toward our dugout. Fortunately, this seemed to do the trick, buying me a few extra minutes of hurried warmup.

As our defense stalled, someone announced we had a special guest for our ceremonial first pitch. Glancing over my shoulder I saw a diminutive old woman, not more than four feet tall, her blonde hair protruding from a white IBL hat. Thinking nothing of her, I began to turn around when the announcer said, "And now, ladies and gentleman, please welcome Ruth Westheimer, the sex doctor!"

"Holy shit!" I thought, momentarily breaking focus. "There she is, *the* sex doctor. And a Jew at that—fantastic!" I turned back around and threw several more warmup pitches, then walked into the tented dugout to dry off.

Partly because everyone remained in the fog of morning, the first three and a half innings flew by. I looked up, and it was 0–0. In the bottom of the fourth, however, a volatile play awoke the entire yard. With two outs and our center fielder, Bryan Langbord, on second, Frankie ripped a sure double to right. Yet due to the shortened fence it played more like a single, forcing Franco to stay at first. But Langbord already decided he was going to score, and, thanks to Jason Rees's outfield gun, the Blue Sox's catcher received the baseball several moments before Bryan got to the plate. .

SMACK!

Langbord trucked the catcher, flattening him. The guy did a nice job holding onto the ball. A good, clean baseball play. Suddenly, the catcher stood over Langbord, talking trash. Langer stood up, they went chest to chest, and dugouts cleared (I refrained from storming the field, instead electing to stand from my chair and shout). There were the normal fuck-yous and get-back-in-your-dugouts, and it dissipated rather quickly. But a significant tone had been set. For lack of a better phrase, it was on. Though the unique circumstances of living, eating, and traveling with other teams had brought everyone closer together, this did not preclude the potential for bad blood. The catcher should have simply flipped the ball to the mound and jogged back to his dugout, even if he was in pain. But his inclination to talk shit revealed something about his understanding of the game. It also heightened the rivalry quickly developing between our two teams.

Bryan returned to the dugout as we readied to take the field. I approached him, trying to figure out exactly what happened since I had been sitting toward the end of the dugout, attempting to stay composed and not lose focus. "What'd he say to you? Want me to dot him? Or I can just hit the first guy."

"Fuck it. Hit him."

Just then from the PA: "We are *sooo* glad everyone is playing together nicely and respecting one another. It would be a shame to see anything *baaad* happen." Was this doofus really admonishing us over the loudspeaker? The absurdity of the comment in a strange way cooled my head, his editorializing bringing me back to earth.

"All right. We'll see," I said to Bryan.

Grabbing my glove, I headed to the mound as Skip grasped my arm. "You're not thinking of doing anything silly, are you?" he said with a characteristic wry grin.

"I'm not sure. It's a close game so probably not."

"No, don't worry about it. Especially not now." Then he added, "Maybe in a couple weeks, when he's not expecting it."

Gangster, I thought, and nodded in approval.

First Half

Warming up there was yet another comment from the PA. This time it was Dr. Ruth. "Now, boys, if you play nice from now on . . . I promise you great sex for the rest of your lives!" Very tempting, but we did not play nice.

Though I decided not to hit the leadoff, trouble would reemerge in the bottom of the sixth. The next time Langbord came to bat, he and the catcher shared a few words. It was clear they were jawing. "Ooh, let me pitch. I want to pitch," the catcher said, intimating that he would pluck Bryan if he was on the mound.

Instead Langbord took out his anger on the baseball, launching an absurdly monstrous home run on the first pitch. He pimped it a bit, flipping his bat high in the air. Our dugout erupted in cheers and taunts. With a two-run homer, the game remained close as I desperately tried to stay calm, focus on the job ahead. No use—I jumped from my seat along with everyone else.

Bryan reached home and exchanged more words with the catcher. "You can pitch. I'll just hit!" As they started to barrel up, both dugouts cleared for a second time. There was much shouting, including by the Blue Sox's catcher, who had the audacity to talk trash to Skip, but each team remained on their side and no punches were thrown. The only saving grace in this altercation was the PA's noticeable absence. A half inning earlier, since the game was taking longer than expected, he said, "Ladies and gentleman, after this inning there will be no more announcing, in preparation for the start of Shabbat."

The next hitter was Wiggy. When the first pitch sailed a foot behind Wigg's head the pitcher should have been ejected immediately. But he did not receive even a warning. We screamed and shouted about what was coming, to no avail. Unsurprisingly, the next pitch struck Wigg in the thigh. Again, not so much as a warning was issued. We came unhinged. If bad blood was simmering before, it now came to a boil. Though no one charged the field, a vendetta was seared into the Lightning's collective psyche, lingering in our minds. It would not be easy to let this one go.

The hardest part about the game was staying calm. Myriad times I felt the urge to hit somebody—as he charged the mound pounding his face, collapsing his zygomatic arch, bloodying him up, cracking his nose, losing his teeth. But this would be (mostly) counterproductive. The best way to beat up on a team was to WIN, silently. In the end I threw a complete game shutout, my first of the season, for a 5–0 victory. It was also nice to learn I'd become the first pitcher in the IBL to reach five wins.

After the game there was yet another interview. But this time it was with a big, black, bald Canadian with huge round sunglasses and a Manny Ramirez T-shirt. Somehow he corralled me and Fish, who had gone three for four at the plate.

"Yo-yo-yo, I'm here with my boys Nate Fish and Aaron Pribble, and they play for the Tel Aviv Lightning. What up, fellas?" It was quickly evident this was not an ordinary interview, more like MTV's *Total Request Live.* Later we found out he was from the ESPN of Canada or something.

"What up, man? We're doing good," Fish replied in his deep Mosaic voice.

"Aw, yeah! You know you doing good, son! That was a big win. You guys looked feisty! Aaron, give me something." He proceeded to bury his big bald head in my shoulder, sticking the mic in my face for an answer.

I wanted to pal around a little but not appear disrespectful toward the Blue Sox, even though their catcher was insolent and their pitcher had just plucked Wiggy. So I opted for the humorous, the sarcastic. "You know, it's a pleasant day. There's a cool breeze, it's not too hot, and we have just a beautiful field here in Tel Aviv—really nice conditions."

"Yeah, yeah, fa sho."

He didn't catch my less than funny Sportek joke, so I went in a different direction, pushed it a bit further. "In fact, Fish has a little jig that he does after each win. Show him, Fish."

"Ha," Fish chuckled gutturally, then proceeded to do something more akin to a capoeira shuffle than a dance. But our interviewer was into it, and he joined along.

After a few more playful questions and answers, we wrapped up. "Yo, you were much funnier than I thought you'd be. Thanks, guys. Good luck this year."

Fish and I walked back to the dugout to grab our stuff before heading to the bus.

"Was that for real?" he said, laughing.

"I'm not sure."

"We almost brawled *and* gave that crazy interview. This league is *nuts*."

"At least the field didn't hurt anybody. That dirt was pretty brutal."

"My dude, I was picking up rocks around third the entire game!"

"And don't forget about Dr. Ruth. Can you believe she was here today? It's too bad we won't have great sex for the rest of our lives; that would be pretty sweet."

"Yeah, but if we'd played nice, the catcher and Langer wouldn't haven't gotten into it."

"And Bryan wouldn't have dropped that BOMB."

"And we might not have won."

"Good point. Who needs Dr. Ruth after all?"

Fish and I looked at each other, both afraid to answer for sure.

18 Rainout in the Desert

Israel's Education Ministry announced Sunday that it had approved a textbook for use in the state's Arab schools that for the first time described Israel's 1948 war of independence as a "catastrophe" for the Arab population. The action, addressing longstanding concerns of the country's Arab population, immediately prompted criticism from right-wing Jewish politicians and calls for the education minister's dismissal.

New York Times, July 22, 2007

"Shit, I can't buy a hit. I'm o for my last 62. What I need is a rainout."

"Rainout? It's hasn't rained in months."

"I can get you a rainout."

"No way!"

"Fifty bucks says I get us a rainout for tomorrow's game."

"You're on, old man. You're on!"

This is how I remember the scene from *Bull Durham*. Journeyman veteran Crash Davis breaks into a Minor League ballpark, hijacks the portable sprinkler system, and proceeds to create a rainout of his own, slipping and sliding with two young rookies on a soaked field in the middle of the night. Needless to say, Crash got his fifty bucks. On the Tel Aviv Lightning, I may have been more akin to Crash Davis than a rookie, but I was no less incredulous that a rainout in Israel was possible.

Since it was another Friday, we arrived at Sportek around eight in the morning to squeeze in our game before the official commencement of Shabbat. Exiting the bus, we noticed two huge puddles at short and second. As we approached the field, our feet sank in wet dirt normally baked solid and firm. Players began to pontificate on the cause of this impending morass.

"Who ever heard of a rainout in the desert?"

"Did it rain last night?"

"Of course, you idiot. How did the puddles get there?"

"Well, it hasn't happened *once* since we've been here."

"Then what about the water?"

"I don't know. Good question."

The pittance of a grounds crew had been working on the field for about an hour. In a perfect world, or even a normal league, each field would have ample tools, giant sponges, sacks of Diamond Dry or Turface. But progress at Sportek was slow since there was all of one rake and a shovel. Like any good ballplayers, we sat around and watched others try to fix the problem. Everyone that is, except for the vigilant Rothem, who was already working with the grounds crew, and Wigg, who hopped up, ripped off his shirt, and ran onto the field in white shorts and flip-flops, lending a hand.

After thirty minutes of work Wigg flopped down in a chair, threw on his shades, put up his feet to sunbathe. Dan continued to toil away. The rest of us did nothing but yak. Someone complained about the lack of Diamond Dry, and someone else noted it would be pointless given the dearth of yearly rain.

Brito mentioned that when it pours in the Dominican, which is often, they just douse the dirt in gasoline and light it on fire. When the gas has burned out, the dirt is dry, the field ready to go. "That's it. *Trenta minutos*, we can play."

Asking around, Fish said they used to do the same thing in Miami, so he and I went hunting. We found some fuel by the concession-stand generator, but the employee wouldn't give us a drop, and the field manager balked at the idea of setting fire to a public park.

"There is no way, no way. Do you want the fire machines to come? I don't think you do," he said indignantly.

An hour later we were increasingly antsy yet only slightly closer to playing. Fixing the field with a rake and a shovel, at a snail's pace, would take until Rosh Hashanah. So Fish and I sneaked behind the concession stand, grabbed the gas can, and dragged it toward the diamond, but were apprehended midway and sternly admonished by the field manager. He was as angry as we were ready to play, so I tried to defuse the situation.

"Okay, you're right. No gas," I said. "Let me tell you a joke to make up for it."

With arms crossed he sighed, unimpressed.

"Good. Here's how it works: I'm going to spell a word, and you're gonna tell me how to say it in English. Like if I spelled *bee-ay-ess-ee-bee-ay-el-el*, you would say . . ."

". . . Baseball."

"Exactly. You got it."

Fish began to grin.

"Okay. Now, how do you say the word *em-ay-cee-dee-oh-en-ay-el-dee-ess?*"

"Mac . . . donald's. McDonald's," he replied.

"Good. And what's *em-ay-cee-eye-en-tee-oh-ess-aych?*"

After a short pause he said, "Macintosh—like the computer!" He was feeling good about his command of the English language.

"Perfect," I said. "Now, this is a tough one. You ready?"

"Yes."

"Okay, now how about *em-ay-cee-aych-eye-en-ee?*"

After a longer pause he answered, "Mac Hine?"

"Oh, close, man. It's actually *machine*, but that's a pretty good try. Two for three is not bad, though. I hope Fish goes two for three at the plate today." Fish tipped back his head and laughed deeply. Fortunately, the crew chief also found this funny. He asked us to please take back the gas, so we did.

Returning from our failed mission, we found our team huddled beneath a small patch of shade behind the dugout, locked in intense debate. Ever since the cafeteria blowup about a lack of security on Opening Day, there were guards at each game. They wore neon-yellow vests with matching bicycle caps and sat in a corner of the yard. Not very intimidating, it was clear their presence was largely for show. Our guard for this game was equally innocuous, except for the silver pistol fastened to his belt.

"That guy's an Arab," said someone flatly.

"So?" said another.

"So? He's an *Arab*, and he's got a gun." This began an unironic debate over whether Arabs should be involved in security and whether Arabs could be Jews. I responded to both in the affirmative but quickly realized the conversation's futility, ducking out early before it devolved into "You're a fool. No, you're a fool." Nonetheless, the concept of an Arab-Israeli security guard was interesting. It added a measure of nuance to our commonly held perceptions about the black-and-white, delineated nature of the region. Further, that an Arab-Israeli security guard might seem to contradict one's inherent notion of security implied that, at least, Arabs could not be trusted with Israel's safety and, at most, all Arabs were terrorist corroborators. Although clearly false, the idea was discernible in statements like, "Arabs shouldn't be able to carry guns" or "Arabs should not be security guards."

We continued to sit in the shade, waiting for a verdict on the field's playability. Time was running out since any game started after 11:30 would risk getting cut short by the beginning of Shabbat. No one enjoyed waking up early for Friday-morning games, but sitting around waiting to play was even worse and guys became increasingly cranky, hostile.

A perceptive manager, Skip sensed this, I think. After using the bathroom he came over to check on us. "Look, guys, you've got to keep it in perspective," he said. We nodded to the beginning of a glass-is-half-full sermon. "We're in Israel, the sun's out, it's a

Friday . . . and I'm taking a dump in a 120-degree Port-o-Potty, sweating my brains out." He cracked a smile, shook his head, and walked away, while we fell from our chairs in laughter. Skip was right—that *was* keeping things in perspective.

Eventually, Commissioner Kurtzer arrived and huddled with the umps and coaches to discuss safety and time constraints. He informed them that the automated sprinkler system had been on the fritz and had not turned off as scheduled. I suspected it was human error in not accounting for our earlier Friday start. Either way, morning games meant less time for the surface to dry, more of a chance something would go wrong. Fortunately, the grounds crew had found some tools. Thanks to their hard work the field looked surprisingly playable. Despite proclamations from several players that they would not play in such dangerous conditions, we were instructed to begin the game at 11:45.

I did not envy Crabb, who was starting on the bump. After sitting for more than three hours in the heat, it's no wonder he did not have his best stuff. Luckily, we were playing Petach Tikva, not a strong hitting team. The Pioneers were throwing a soft lefty, and Skip exhorted our hitters to stay back, let the ball travel. The best executor of this strategy was Jeff, who hit a beautiful opposite-field bomb to left, sans grunt. And Fish went two for three, just like the field manager.

In the sixth inning the announcer said, "Now batting for the Lightning is number 14, left fielder Josh Matlow. He will be the last hitter announced for the game since I have to turn off the electricity in preparation for Shabbat. *Toda.*" The game continued, and we finished without him, drawing ever closer to the beginning of the Day of Rest. Crabb battled and threw strikes for an 8–3 victory. In the end, the conditions at Sportek were no worse than usual. There were bumps and bad hops but no exceptional misfortunes on this ordinarily unordinary field. At least no one broke an ankle or was hit in the head.

First Half

If I were Crash Davis I would have lost my fifty bucks. It was a rain *delay*, not a rain*out*, in the desert. But Crash was a fictional character on a Minor League team in a movie. I was a real-life player turned teacher turned player, competing in Israel's first-ever professional baseball league.

19 Blooming the Desert

SEVERAL MORNINGS LATER WE ATTENDED A TREE-
planting ceremony sponsored by the Jewish National Fund in
Modi'in. (The JNF was a chief sponsor of the league, their blue
and green logo appearing on the right sleeve of each jersey.)
Since buses were supposed to depart at 8:45, Andrew commenced
banging on doors sometime earlier in hopes of rousting players
from their slumber. About half the league responded. During the
early-morning transit I wondered if we were heading to Modi'in
proper, or Modi'in Illit. The former is a historical and contemporary Israeli city, the latter a West Bank settlement positioned
between Tel Aviv and Jerusalem.

Planting trees in Israel is a time-honored tradition, a means
of turning the desert green, helping transform a once parched,
windswept landscape into a more hospitable, verdant environment. For the Diaspora, purchasing trees was an act of patriotism,
loyalty, deference to those brothers and sisters living the dream in
a Jewish homeland. But, like everything in the Land of Dueling

Narratives, there was a flip side to this story. Some claimed trees were planted to conceal long-standing Arab villages razed after the war of 1948. Rothem was the first to argue in my presence this perspective (or plant the seed, as it were). What better way to deny a people's sovereign claims than to destroy its evidence by reverting the land to epochs prior? It made sense: enshroud in national myth the bald realities of struggle, and for the sake of some larger goal sweep regrettable events under the carpet of history. Collateral damage, perhaps, but one could not say with certainty. More likely, it seemed, both truths were correct. Not every tree in Israel masked a flattened Arab village; surely, many were planted on land previously void of human and vegetative life. For reasons just and unjust alike, it was clear Israel would not be the nation it is today without the eager financial support and manual labor of those committed to transforming vision into reality.

Thus I rolled in, as usual, with conflicting emotions. Small towns were visible in the distance, and though Modi'in was not in sight, it may have been close by. Situated among rolling hills spotted with distinctive pale stone outcroppings and sporadic packs of trees was a bucolic biblical re-creation. We alighted from the bus wearing hats, jerseys, and a mélange of khaki and athletic shorts and descended a cement trail past small ponds, frond-covered benches, water mills, vibrant arbors with high-hanging bells, timber engraved with biblical passages in Hebrew and English: From the Fig Tree Comes the Fig (Somebody 4:16) and Work the Soil to Fill the Land (Someone Else 3:23). It was like the Middle Eastern version of an old western movie set—a simulacrum. I would not be surprised to have learned of a subterranean shopping mall, or that the surrounding pomegranate trees were in fact plastic.

We gathered in a covered amphitheater at the basin of the grounds. Two JNF *machers* were preaching about the symbolism of planting trees, like baseball, in Israel, watching them grow side by side. There was talk of resettling the land and a healthy quoting of the Torah. It made me uneasy. When Rothem heard the name of our specific location he grumbled half audibly about there being old Arab villages here, about not so much as recognizing their existence. Then they passed around cups of wine, calling for us to say a tree prayer. *"Baruch Ata Adonai . . . ,"* it began.

Leaning in close, Rothem warned me that the elixir came from a Jewish winery in Arab East Jerusalem, on occupied land. He respectfully declined a cup. *"Lo, toda."*

I reluctantly accepted. Apprehensive, when time to drink I poured the red liquid onto the earth, like a 1990s hip-hop video, for those fallen homeboys in need of a taste.

Rothem missed this devious act of rebellion. "Traitor," he said disapprovingly.

I shook my head, motioned to the ground below me, and gave a surreptitious wink. Slightly curling the left side of his mouth, Dan countered with a subtle smile.

After donning JNF hats for a group snapshot, we ascended a dirt path into the hills, reaching a clearing. Shovels, semidug plots, and almond saplings awaited us. We learned almonds were the most durable and hardest working of trees, that they were the first to bloom, could survive a drought to blossom anew six months later. Yes, the symbolism was rich.

The Dominicans jumped in wholeheartedly, hooting and hollering, playing in the dirt. From our newly elevated location the panorama was exquisite. Hills and valleys stretched out in front of us. I grabbed the essentials, walked alone toward the side of the hill, and found a plot. Since holes were already dug, the work was easy, negligible. Resting the plantlet in its earthen vessel, I covered it with dirt, soaked it with water, and placed a semicircle of rocks around the edge: a personal touch. As the arboreal chain gang rumbled behind me, I gazed into the distance. Greening the land, helping beautify the state of Israel was a worthy endeavor, a deed in which I was proud to partake.

But the notion of concealing since-demolished Arab villages, of contributing to an illicit settlement, troubled my thoughts. I searched the distance for answers, but there were none, only a light breeze cutting through the morning heat. At once troubled and satisfied with my work, I resumed watering the fresh tree.

Just then Rothem came trudging down the hill. "That's the West Bank, you know."

"Where—here?" Oh, no, I was a collaborator.

"No—out there." Dan said the JNF was careful not to plant over the Green Line, that in fact a row of trees in the middle distance separated Palestine from Israel.

Just barely visible atop a hill to our left was a road that served as the Separation Wall. We were merely a half mile away, yet one would never know. Staring at the handsome terrain, political boundaries disappeared. The dry grass rustled. A snake slid beneath the cool belly of a rock. Trees swayed with satisfaction. And somewhere in the valley, a bird of prey took flight. On either side of the road, in Israel and Palestine, the land itself remained the same.

20 Bus Ride

The leader of Hezbollah, Sheik Hassan Nasrallah, said his militia's rockets could reach all of Israel, including Tel Aviv. Mr. Nasrallah has previously said that the group could have fired on Tel Aviv in its war with Israel last summer.

New York Times, July 24, 2007

I WAS TRYING TO STAY FOCUSED FOR MY FIRST START against the Modi'in Miracle, whose orange and blue uniforms were modeled after the New York Mets, except the cityscape on the Mets' logo was replaced with a Menorah on Modi'in's, which was especially fitting since they were managed by famed Jewish Met outfielder Art Shamsky. We were up two on the Miracle—two behind Bet Shemesh—and since this was a doubleheader, much was at stake.

As the bus rambled toward the field, however, my thoughts kept drifting to the scene in the distance. Though pasty brown, the hills appeared somehow white, like a blank canvas on which to lay my impressions of this foreign land. I wondered if I would ever make it to Palestine, if the people would accept me, if it was too dangerous. And except for the cryptic Arabic instructions from the merchant in the Muslim Quarter of Jerusalem a month earlier, I had no idea how, if ever, I would get there.

Arriving at Kibbutz Gezer, a.k.a. the Geez, we cut across fields of sunflowers, through the obligatory security gate, down a dirt road, past some houses, before reaching the softball field. The softball field? We heard about the Geez's odd configurations, but it was a shock nonetheless. The miniature infield housed ninety-foot bases placed just short of the outfield grass. The warning track for the softball field, a thick strip of dirt, arced across the middle of the outfield about a hundred feet from the recently extended fence, which was now sitting up a five-foot hill. And there was a light pole in the middle of right field. Seriously. Not to worry, though, someone had duct-taped a mattress to the pole lest an ambitious outfielder should actually decide to attempt making a play.

Stepping down from the bus, guys were kvetching at full throttle.

"Can you believe this?"

"What a joke!"

"More like the Israel *Bush* League."

Since I was starting I let everyone exit first, taking my time to leave. I looked out past the spectacle of the field onto a sea of sunflowers. Brittle and withered, their ordinarily bright faces, now prostrated and sullen, left a striking impression. I wondered if they faced down in shame from the substandard playing conditions, in honor of our presence, or in disgust at our attempt to bring baseball to this holy land. And hallowed it was. Some legends claimed that past the sunflowers in left, at the foot of a modest slope, lay the tomb of King Solomon, son of David and once ruler of the Kingdom of Israel. Large white alabaster stones canopied with black archaeological tenting protruded regally from the otherwise sparse landscape. It appeared the king and his sunflower foot soldiers were posthumously observing our every move. Though we would have only twenty to thirty fans in attendance, it was clear I was pitching for a much larger audience.

Warming up in the bullpen, or rather the side of a hill in left, I noticed Maximo Nelson strolling down the line to get loose as well. Evidently, today's battle for second place would feature a high school history teacher versus a six-foot-eight flamethrowing Dominican. If the PA guy showed up, I hoped he wouldn't announce it as such.

In the first inning both teams scored a run. Ours was an RBI single from Fish, and theirs came on an Eladio Rodriguez home run. Eladio was one of the top two or three hitters in the league. He carried himself with a mixture of arrogance and grace, exuding professionalism, which was no surprise given his Minor League experience with the Boston Red Sox.

Great player or not, Eladio's first homer was cheap. I threw him an 0-1 fastball away, which he popped 290 feet to right. Jeff was already playing behind the light pole, up the hill, with his back against the 280-foot fence. The ball waterfalled just over his glove to tie the score in the first.

It would remain 1–1 until the fifth. With two on and one out, Modi'in's first baseman popped to shallow left. From shortstop El Ave flew back, camped underneath. Our left fielder called him off but misjudged the pop-up, which dropped between the two of them to load the bases. I thought briefly about whether the play would be ruled a hit or an error. After a strikeout, Eladio once again strolled to the plate. With two balls and one strike I threw a change, knowing he was looking to go big fly with the bags loaded, thinking he would jump at the off-speed. He did just that, except the pitch was closer to his belt than his knees. Sufficiently ahead of the change, he was nonetheless able to make good contact given the pitch's height. He hit another pop-up, this time to left. Our left fielder ran up the hill and pressed against the fence. The ball landed just over his outstretched glove for a grand slam and Eladio's second home run.

We ended up losing 5–3. In the second game Eladio hit two more home runs (both legit), propelling the Miracle to another victory, placing them alone in second place and dropping us to third. It wasn't right to deny Eladio his props, but it was also safe to say we were hurt by the Geez. I knew in the long run it would probably all even out, but that sentiment was of little comfort in the short run.

It was my first loss of the year. To be honest, I forgot what it felt like. My last loss came three years earlier in France, and I was having trouble making sense of the emotions. Searching for some solace, if only an act of denial, I could blame a portion of the outcome on the short, bizarre field. I was thus far undefeated and had been throwing well; now I was 5-1. Then there was the matter of my ERA. I wondered if all five runs were earned and thought only two should have been. After the mishap in left I heard the scorer lean over to the Modi'in bench and say, "What do you think, hit or error?"

"Oh, give it a hit!" the bench said emphatically. If it was my team, I'd have said the same thing. But it wasn't. So that was five big ones in the wrong column. I could probably go talk to someone about changing it, which players here did all the time, but then I'd be a fucking stat rat just like the rest of them. Probably a natural tendency, it still wasn't right. Plus the move went against my mantra: process over product.

This maxim applied to baseball and life. The best way to get positive results was to focus on the doing, the how. Just keep your head down, work hard, and look up at the end to see where you are. I first learned this lesson in Miss Murphy's ninth-grade Art Explorations class. On the wall was an eccentric handmade poster emblazoned with three words: *process over product*. I glanced up one day, and it just clicked. Will I get an A on my painting? Just work hard, and it will be fine. Will I have a good ERA? Just focus on throwing strikes down in the zone, and you'll get there. It's not even that the product is unimportant. It is important. Rather, the best way to achieve one's goal is to concentrate on *how* to get there. Hence process over product. Hence the reason I don't read the paper or look at my stats until after the season. So fuck the stats and the losses for today. Let's get back on the bus.

Sometimes the ride home takes an instant; this day it took forever. Perhaps I was overly pensive after the loss, but pulling away from the game I noticed the setting sun. It was a large bloodred orb, casting a rosy glow on the hills of the West Bank behind us in the distance. Rays of light shone through filmy bus windows as the sun neared impact with a looming horizon. I thought of the largely impoverished Arabs in the West Bank, of King Solomon and his Israelite progeny. Who cared about baseball when this centuries-old conflict was still raging? If baseball couldn't help unite these two lands, what good was it?

Staring out the window, I lost track of space and time. Suddenly I was back in France. During a trip from Paris to our home in Toulouse, I mused that for all intents and purposes we could have been on a bus in West Texas, where I played the summer before, as the view was identical. A yellow line raced beside us in the foreground, followed by metronoming telephone poles and a steadfast plain in the distance, illuminated only by the faint light of a fading sun.

In a vain attempt to be like my dad, who was a working musician until I was born, I remembered the hook to a song I once tried to write:

Staring out the window the miles pass on by
As France merges into Texas in the twilight sky
It's just another long bus ride.

How many times, under how many conditions, in how many places, had I ridden the bus? Whatever the final tally, I could add to the song one more verse:

As I dream of peace in Israel and Palestine
It's just another long bus ride, it's just another long bus ride
It's just another long bus ride.

21 Three Fields of Wheat

I DIDN'T RECOGNIZE THE NUMBER ON MY CELL PHONE but decided to answer it anyway: "Hello?"

"Hi, *Aron*."

"Hey. Who's this?" It was a female voice, whose I couldn't tell.

"*Aron*, how are you?"

"Good—but who is this?"

"This is Yael."

I was caught off guard. "Yael? Oh, hey, Yael." Nice of her to call me long distance. "Um, how's Germany?"

"Germany?" She paused. "*Aron*, I have something to tell you. I did not go to Germany."

"What? Did your flight get delayed or something? That was like three weeks ago."

"*Aron*, I never went."

"When are you going?"

"I am not going to Germany."

"Then where are you going?"

"No—*Aron*, I did not go to Germany; I'm not going anywhere. Can we talk in person? I think this is better."

"Okay."

"Now, if you are available."

"Yeah, it's Saturday, so we don't have a game. Why don't you come pick me up at the *kfar*, and we can go somewhere to talk . . . There's this cool little café on Shenkin Street in Tel Aviv."

I hung up and went to the basketball court, shooing several nosy peacocks to scavenge the laundry heaps for some respectable clothes. If she didn't go to Germany, where had she been? Shit, she was married and left her husband. I had made a cuckold of some poor Israeli. No, she said she lived with her folks. Maybe she just had a boyfriend. But if she'd been in Israel this whole time, why the hell was she calling me now? Who knew.

When she pulled up in the little red Peugeot I felt butterflies excitedly return. I had pushed her out of my mind, thinking she was gone for good. Upon seeing her, the emotions came rushing back.

Instead of a café we went to a small park canopied by trees, near the water. Sitting on a bench, Yael explained that although she really did have a sister living in Germany, she had lied about going to stay with her. "I was scared to meet an American. You said you were just here for the summer, and I did not know what to do. Plus, you tried to kiss me around all those animals and we had just met, so I made up a story."

"Good story."

"Thank you."

"So why did you decide to call me back?"

She grinned.

"Well?"

"I said I was scared. I did not say I was not interested."

"Maybe *I'm* not interested anymore." I tried to play it cool. "Maybe."

We spent the day meandering through the streets of Tel Aviv, walking nowhere in particular. We got smoothies at a ubiquitous outdoor fruit stand, walked along the beach until it became too hot, slipped down quiet side streets past bougainvilleas and plumeria trees. Ducking into trendy, air-conditioned boutiques, we made fun of passersby. I found it amusing that a young Hasidic Jew in fur hat and trench coat would be carrying a skateboard, that a bodybuilder inked head to toe in tattoos would also be holding a yarmulke (though Yael seemed to think this was completely normal). More than anything, it was just good to spend time together.

We were both getting hungry from all the walking and talking, so we headed to Dizengoff Center, the biggest mall in Tel Aviv. Standing just outside the complex she asked, "Do you see this intersection?"

"Yes."

"This is where we had one of the most deadly *piguas*. When I was in secondary school a terrorist blew himself up on a bus right here in the middle of the day, when the streets were busiest. Many people died."

"Shit."

"I remember watching on TV, and there was a head rolling across the sidewalk." She pointed to the striped white lines at our feet. "This I will never forget."

I told her when I was in Israel on Birthright two years ago, I was afraid to ride buses for this reason. Instead I walked or took taxis, figured they had less chance of exploding. U.S. newspapers were headlined with macabre events of the Middle East, and this, more than anything, is what the majority of Americans associated with Israel. This time around, however, the thought of a suicide bombing did not occur to me, was not present in my thoughts. Or perhaps I had just accepted the outside possibility of a *pigua* as something that came with life in Israel. There would always be a measure of death and violence here, I said. It seemed par for the course. Yael did not disagree, noting that earlier in the day we had walked past the site where former prime minister Yitzhak Rabin was assassinated, by a Jew.

This seemed like heavy conversation for a burgeoning relationship, and I did not want to make it weird. But Yael had opened the door, and I couldn't resist a bit more cultural investigation. This was part of the attraction, along with her majestically wavy black hair.

"So, this might sound strange, but I've been wondering . . ." Tread lightly, Pribble. "You said your family is from Yemen, right?"

"Yes."

"But you're Jewish."

"Of course."

"But Yemen is considered an Arabic country."

"Yes, but there are Jews there too."

"So can Jews be Arabs?"

"No, of course not."

"Why?"

"Because we are *Jews*."

"Well, what language did your grandparents speak?"

"Hebrew."

"But they emigrated from Yemen, right? So they also spoke Arabic, or Judeo-Arabic."

"Yes, but it was not their first language. Anyway, we are not Arabs, we are *Jews*." I wanted to ask her again why she couldn't be both, why they were mutually exclusive, but the force with which she proclaimed her identity suggested otherwise. So I left it alone as we entered the tall glass facade of Dizengoff Center to grab lunch.

Inside, sitting somewhat awkwardly alongside a slender, graceful Yemenite, I thought of the many different Jews we had encountered: white, brown, light, dark; short, tall, big, skinny; hirsute, pretty, funny, scary; gay, straight, rich, poor. Jews in the land of our forefathers, so many varieties, shapes, and sizes, a mélange so very different from our commonly held perceptions and stereotypes. Perhaps there was room for an interloper, a haole, a redneck Jew-boy such as myself, under this beautiful Hebrew rainbow.

We hung out the very next night after our game. Since we had spent time in Tel Aviv on two occasions, we drove just north of the city to the harbor in Herzliya, a town named after the founder of modern Zionism, the movement to re-create a homeland for the Jewish people, Theodor Herzl. The harbor featured a lively promenade straddled by restaurants strung with white lights on one side, a boat dock on the other. Yael and I sat adjacent to one another at an outdoor table overlooking the sea.

Stars stubborn enough to shine through the ambient glow of the wharf blended with boat lights in the distance. It was a pleasant night, if still hot, and I was in good spirits after our win against Netanya earlier in the evening. Contrasting with the previous day, our conversation was pedestrian yet entertaining. We talked about favorite movies, favorite types of music, and favorite foods, squabbling about ketchup versus mustard, vanilla versus chocolate, and the proper way to cut one's pancakes. We could have been talking about anything. It only mattered that I was close enough to bump her leg when she said something funny, grab her hand for brief moments at a time.

Afterward we walked to a pier at the end of the harbor, where lights from the promenade had all but disappeared. It was just us. We could hear the birds and smell the sea but see neither; only the stars and lights from the occasional boat were visible.

"*Aron*, how many fields of wheat do you have?"

I had clearly misheard. "I think you just asked how many fields of wheat I have. Is that like a saying in Hebrew or something? It doesn't really translate well."

"No, this is what I mean: how many fields of wheat?"

"Like metaphorically?"

"No, literally."

"I *literally* have zero fields of wheat."

"Then it will never work between us."

"What?"

She smirked.

"Wipe that look off your face and tell me what the hell you're talking about."

"Well, my grandpa, who grew up in Yemen, always used to say I needed to find a good man to marry. A man who could take care of me, who was well-off. A man, he said, who had three fields of wheat."

"Well, I don't have three fields of wheat. Guess I'm out of luck."

"I guess you are."

I picked up the hair falling over the front of her shoulder and curled it around my fingers, looking into her eyes. "Well, then I'd better make the most of my opportunity. I'm not gonna wait for some wealthy farmer to come sweep you off your feet."

"Yes, I think you should."

I leaned in for a kiss. Fortunately, this time Yael did not pull away.

22 Losing Sucks

A 20-year-old Palestinian man died after an Israeli soldier hit him with a baton at a checkpoint near Bethlehem. The army spokeswoman said that the man had drawn a knife and that a soldier hit him after another soldier fell in a scuffle.

New York Times, July 26, 2007

LET ME KVETCH A BIT: TODAY THERE WAS NO ROSIN bag on the mound. This may seem innocuous and I may sound like a prima donna for bringing it up, but I don't care.

Since afternoons at Sportek were miserably humid, one might think morning games would be better. However, the combination of dew and rapidly climbing heat produced a ludicrous level of moisture in the air. In the first inning my cap was dripping like a faucet. Sweat trickled off my left arm, down my hand. The ump said I could not bring a towel to the mound, so twice I called time and walked to the dugout to dry myself off. My left hip, normally a sweaty hand's refuge, was already wet, so I began wiping my socks and inner thigh in search of a dry spot, caressing my crotch in an unflattering gesticulation. Like I said, today there was no rosin bag on the mound.

As may already be apparent, the game did not start well. Adding to the sweat, I had below-average, erratic stuff. To make matters worse, we were playing Modi'in, the team responsible for my first loss of the season and our slide into third place. At some point in the first inning I mumbled, "Well, the ball's gonna go where it's gonna go, and that's it." I started throwing instead of pitching. Strangely enough this seemed to work, but not before giving up three runs on three walks, a single, and a couple of infield ground outs. It was not going well.

After the first the wetness was controllable, but my location was not. I gave up only one run over the next three innings, but each was a struggle. Fortunately, our hitters battled back to put the score at 4–4 in the fourth. But in the fifth I gave up two more runs on another walk and a pop-up homer just beyond Sportek's short porch in right. The bomb was cheap, but I hung a change-up, so the results were deserved. Plus, I walked yet another guy, for which there is no excuse.

In the sixth I hit the first batter, and Skip pulled me. Several innings earlier, when I faced the same hitter, I barked at him for standing too close to the plate while I was warming up. He had violated one of the most important unwritten rules of baseball: never stand too close to the batter's box between innings. Assuredly every ballplayer knew this gave the hitter an unfair look at what the pitcher was throwing. So when the batter, who happened to be Israeli, stood just outside the box as I was getting loose, I figured he was showing me up. Plus, I was testy.

"You better back the fuck up or you're gonna get it in the ribs."

He didn't hear me, asked Wigg behind the dish what I was saying. "You're right up close to the plate, and he's warming up. Give him some fucking room, mate!"

"But I wasn't in the batter's box!" The Israeli didn't have a clue. Was he supposed to have a clue? Probably not, because one with such little experience couldn't be expected to understand the intimacies of the game, but I wasn't thinking logically. Pitching poorly, I was running on fumes while trying to keep our squad in the game.

When he came up next time, to lead off the sixth, I fell behind 1-0 on a fastball down and away. I thought, "This guy sucks and he's a lefty. You've got the advantage—just throw him cock shots. You *cannot* walk the ninth hitter." So I let up and tried to groove one, slowing down my arm, dragging it behind me. This caused the pitch to sail up and in, which coincided with the square of his back. I did not try to hit him, of course, because we were at this point down 6–5. But I had, after threatening to do just that innings earlier, and Skip gave me the hook.

We ended up losing 9–8. Our hitters battled the entire way, but I let them down. It was a terrible defeat. In the games since my last start we had battled back, but now Modi'in was tied with us for second, while Bet Shemesh was still three games ahead in first.

During my arm troubles at the start of the season I thought being hurt was worse than playing bad. Now I wasn't so sure. This second loss felt much worse. I had thrown poorly, and it was a tough one to swallow. In our postgame meeting Skip mentioned that I had to let it go, move on, flush it. But sometimes you can't flush it. You try, but the handle gets stuck and the water keeps running. Then you wake up in the middle of the night to jiggle the thing, but it's no use. The water continues to run. It keeps you up, eating incessantly at the back of your mind. Then it shoots to the forefront of your thoughts and your heart starts racing, yet the game has been over for hours, days. You try to suppress the anger, push away the fury. It travels, sits in your stomach like a black hole, an infinitely dense nothing, sucking everything around it into an abyss of despair.

When I was young I had a ridiculous temper. If I so much as walked a guy in Little League I would cry on the mound. If I gave up a few hits and heaven forbid a few runs, I would charge into the dugout, throw my glove against the fence, tears pouring down my face, pouting. When I got home I'd continue blubbering. I'd dream about smashing a lamp with my bat, or putting my fist through a pane of glass. At one point when I was eleven, sobbing on the drive home after a loss, my dad had finally heard enough. He slammed on the brakes, laying twenty feet of rubber behind us in the middle of the road. In so many words, he told me to shut up and stop being a baby. He was right. Though the crying stopped just in time to start high school, the feeling inside never went away.

This sensation, which my dad called the inner fire, is both good and bad. It's the same energy that propels you to work tirelessly in the off-season, pumps you up for big starts, and helps you bear down on the leadoff hitter in the last inning of a tie game. But it also spills over, has you cussing at your middle infielders in the seventh against Bet Shemesh about a double play that should have been turned. It's also what makes you übercompetitive, for better and worse. Sometimes when it gets out of control it makes you cry yourself to sleep at age eleven, with a throbbing headache, because the flame has burned out and there is nothing left in you. Sometimes as a sophomore in high school you wonder if it's all worth it, because you want it so fucking much but it takes so much out of you, is so totally and wholly life consuming. Then you feel bad about yourself for even thinking that.

Sometimes you're all grown up, but you still sense that black hole like a pit in your stomach. You try to stay cool and root for your teammates, though not too much because you don't want to look like you're cheering just to get out of the inning, saving your ERA. But not too little, either, because you don't want to appear as if you've given up. You haven't felt this way in years, but it's the same as ever. Part of you wants to throw your glove, scream at the umpire, knock over the water cooler, put your foot through the shitty plastic gardening chairs sorely substituting for a dugout bench, rip down the blue tarp poorly doubling for a dugout wall, snap a bat over your knee, and rip up a knuckle as you unleash on the chain-link fence in front of your face. FUCK! But instead you just walk off the mound after hitting the first batter of the sixth inning in the middle of the desert. Maybe you cross your legs, or maybe you just sit there. You grab a towel, dry your arms, and take a deep breath. All this time the fire inside is waiting for the next dose of oxygen. It gets its fuel, flickers, grows stronger, and comes roaring back. The fire radiates down your arm, and you open and clench your fist, staring at it intently. Exasperated, you loosen your grip, place your hand palm down on your knee, take another breath. On the outside you try to keep a calm facade, but on the inside you're that eleven-year-old kid, throwing a tantrum.

After the game on the bus ride home you try to stay even-keeled because you know it's a long season, but ball four or the hanging change keeps popping into your mind. You try to jiggle the handle, but the toilet is clogged, not flushing. You just got your second loss, and, more important, you just gave up second place. And now you're supposed to have a fun All-Star Weekend? Good luck. Losing *sucks*.

1. The peacocks of Kfar Hayarok. Courtesy of Jacob Levy.

2. *Far left*: Dan Rothem, Stuart Brito, and Adam Crabb on Opening Day at Yarkon Field. Courtesy of Jacob Levy.

3. *From right*: Jeff Hastings, Nate Fish, Bryan
Langbord, and Aaron Pribble hanging in Fish's
dorm room. Courtesy of Jacob Levy.

4. Aaron Pribble being interviewed at Yarkon
Field after a win over the Petach Tikva Pioneers.
Courtesy of Jacob Levy.

5. Hector De Los Santos, a.k.a. Matacaballo,
dining in the caf. Courtesy of Jacob Levy.

6. Rafael Rojano rides a camel at the Mount of Olives in Jerusalem. Courtesy of the author.

7. Daniel Kurtzer (*left*) and Alan Gardner
(*far right*) and other players at the near-strike
contract negotiations at Kfar Hayarok. Courtesy
of Jacob Levy.

8. Dane Wigg during the contract negotiations
at Kfar Hayarok. Courtesy of Jacob Levy.

9. Jacob Levy beside the teams' laundry heaps at Kfar Hayarok. Courtesy of Jacob Levy.

10. The Tel Aviv Lightning versus the Bet Shemesh Blue Sox at Sportek. Courtesy of the author.

11. Nate Fish with a goat at the Kfar Hayarok petting zoo. Courtesy of the author.

12. *From left*: Jamie Aimar, Dane Wigg, Aaron Pribble, Jason Rees, John Thew, and Adam Crabb atop Masada. Courtesy of the author.

13. Approaching an Israeli security
barrier in the West Bank. Courtesy of
the author.

14. The Tel Aviv Lightning All-Stars. *Top row, from left*: Nate Fish, Aaron Pribble, Adam Crabb, Dan Rothem, Steve Hertz, Stuart Brito, and Jeff Hastings. *Bottom row, from left*: Dane Wigg, Josh Matlow, Matt Brill, Raul Franco, and Dan Kaufman. Courtesy of the author.

15. Dan Rothem and the Tel Aviv Lightning
batboy, Yotam, at the All-Star Game. Courtesy
of Jacob Levy.

16. Stuart "Pupo" Brito at the All-Star Game.
Courtesy of Jacob Levy.

17. The Dominicans and friends at the All-Star Game. Courtesy of Jacob Levy.

18. Eladio Rodriguez and Juan Feliciano at the
All-Star Game. Courtesy of Jacob Levy.

19. Raul "El Ave" Franco at Kibbutz Gezer.
Courtesy of the author.

20. The Tel Aviv Lightning versus the Modi'in Miracle at Kibbutz Gezer. Moko Moanaroa is in left field. Courtesy of the author.

21. Israeli police survey the West Bank.
Courtesy of the author.

22. Shopping in the Muslim Quarter in
Jerusalem. Courtesy of the author.

23. Entering the city of Ramallah. Courtesy of
the author.

24. Boys playing catch in Ramallah. Courtesy of the author.

25. Approaching the Wall of Separation and an
Israeli checkpoint from the West Bank. Courtesy
of the author.

26. *From left*: Jeff Hastings, Adam Crabb, Nate
Fish, and Aaron Pribble following a playoff loss
to the Modi'in Miracle at Sportek. It was the
Tel Aviv Lightning's final game of the season.
Courtesy of Jacob Levy.

27. *From left*: Aaron Rosdal, Bryan Langbord,
and Nate Fish at Kfar Hayarok preparing for the
Schnitzel Awards. Courtesy of Jacob Levy.

28. Dane Wigg and Steve Hertz at Kfar
Hayarok after the Schnitzel Awards. Courtesy of
Jacob Levy.

29. Bet Shemesh, the IBL Champions, at Yarkon
Field. Courtesy of Jacob Levy.

ALL-STAR BREAK

23 Flirting with Ramallah

WHAT'S THE BEST WAY TO FLUSH IT? GO HAVE some fun. Or better yet, scare the heck out of yourself, forget about your performance, and be grateful that you're still around to pitch another day.

It was the night after our loss to Modi'in. Since we had two days off for the All-Star break, some of us talked about going to Masada and the Dead Sea. But our plans were vague at best. We figured all that was needed were directions and a couple of vehicles. So while Crabb, Jeff, and Wigg went to Ben-Gurion Airport to rent cars, I called Yael to find out how to get there.

"You are going by yourselves? This is crazy. It is very dark, and the road is dangerous. People crash there all the time. Who is the Israeli that will take you?"

"We don't have an Israeli. It's only us. We were just gonna rent a couple cars and head out."

"Oh, no, this is unacceptable. You *must* have someone to take you there."

"Really? Nobody we know can go, and this is like our only chance. I think we gotta do it."

Yael sighed deeply. "Well, if you must, I will call my father. I hope he is not sleeping. He knows the roads like the back of his hand."

Eventually she called back to relay directions, which I scribbled on a sheet of yellow lined paper. They read:

> Take Road 1 to Jerusalem. When you enter the city, you will see a sign that says Sakharov Gardens. Shortly after will be a sign to the Dead Sea. Take it to the left. You will then reach a checkpoint. DO NOT GO STRAIGHT—THIS IS RAMALLAH. At the checkpoint, go right. Take this road until it T-bones and turn right again. Follow it all the way south until you reach Masada and the Dead Sea.

Yael made sure to emphasize that the West Bank was very dangerous and that we needed to stay out. She said there were also sinkholes along the way, and, to make matters worse, travel warnings were being posted due to Saturday's projected temperature of 110 degrees. "Call me when you arrive. I want to know you are not dead."

"I don't like the dead part. How about, 'Call me so I know you're alive'?"

"Okay. Call me so I know you are not dead."

"I just said—fine, I'll call." I was starting to have second thoughts. I wanted to explore Masada and the Dead Sea, and eventually wished to travel to Ramallah. But I wasn't ready to visit the latter in the middle of the night with zero preparation, though I couldn't very well back out at this point, either.

We had been up for many hours, procrastinating, waffling on whether to go. By the time the guys got back from the airport, having driven thirty minutes in the opposite direction toward Gaza, nearly reaching the Strip unintentionally, it was late into the night, and most everyone, it seemed, was asleep. When we finally packed up and prepared to leave it was three thirty in the morning. Ordinarily, our late start would not have been a big deal, except we were on a mission to see the sunrise at Masada. Since it took about two hours to get there and sunrise began around five thirty, we were cutting it close. I sat shotgun in one car, with Crabb and Jason Rees in the back and Jeff driving. Wiggy took the other car, carrying two Aussies, Johnny Thew and the Modi'in lefty Matt Bennett, as well as a southerner named Jamie. Little did we know, this was Wiggy's first time driving outside of Australia, and thus his first experience driving on the right side of the road.

Out of the *kfar* we jumped on Road 5 as if heading to Yarkon. Not a moment later Wiggy shot out from behind us, speeding down the highway, despite the fact that I carried the only directions. Merging onto Road 4 we then took the Road 1 exit to Jerusalem. We drove for miles, but Wiggy was nowhere in sight. Suddenly, we received a barrage of frantic calls and texts from the missing car, asking where to go. But as we had not been driving at the same excessive speed, we were far behind and had no idea where they were.

For the next hour our cars excruciatingly crisscrossed Jerusalem in search of each other and the Dead Sea exit, until we discovered there were in fact two Road 1s: one red and one blue. Seriously. After we backtracked several times, Rees spotted a small sign on Red Road 1, near Sakharov Gardens in the opposite direction. Though we still did not know the location of the other car, we followed the sign anyway. Wigg would just have to figure it out and catch up.

As we took the exit and headed off the main road, we thought our troubles were over. Yet they had only just begun. Things got very suspicious. Orange signs began to appear in English, Hebrew, and Arabic: DANGER! WARNING! CHANGE OF DRIVING ROUTE!

We were traveling along the Wall of Separation. The farther we went, the darker the road became, with fewer signs, increased fortifications. There were large gray walls on either side of the road and no indication of life. Yael had said nothing about this, only that it was a dangerous route. Scouring the directions, I looked for any mention of such alien terrain.

The car was silent, and no one knew what to expect. We continued down the path, through a tunnel, and took a sharp left past a roundabout, encountering a checkpoint directly in front of us. It was something of a giant tollbooth, with a large metal overhang stretching to the other side of the road, bright lights shining on the cars below. On one side heavily armed soldiers—Israeli or Palestinian, we couldn't tell—were stopping what few cars were on the road at four in the morning, instructing passengers to get out, open their trunks, and be searched. On our side there was nothing.

Approaching the checkpoint, Jeff slowed down to look for the right-hand turn as Yael had instructed, but there was no place to go. So he continued straight. It was all happening in slow motion, yet much too quickly. Jeff was rolling through the checkpoint, in spite of Yael's exhortation *not* to under any circumstances. As he did we awoke from our torpor, the inside of the car erupting in a cacophony of fits and howls.

"We're going through! Noooooo!"

"Where are we?"

"Which way are we going? This is Ramallah—turn around!"

No one knew what to do, and Jeff was driving no more than five miles an hour. Just as he crossed the threshold, Crabb yelled out, "For fuck's sake, mate, STOP! I'm not going into Ramallah! Stop! Back up! Shit!"

"Dude, back up, back up. Do it, man." I did not want to proceed either.

In a hurry Jeff reversed through the checkpoint and back up the road, swerving past intermittent cars traveling in the proper direction. Just then, someone stopped behind us, turned off their lights, pulled slowly along our left side. We held our breath in frantic anticipation. Were we about to get hijacked? Was it Shabak, Mossad? What did this damn car want?

"Oy, fellas. What the hell ya doing?" rang a sharp Aussie accent from the driver seat. Sitting shotgun, Bennett was drinking a Red Bull and smoking a cigarette. In the back seat Thew was playing video games, propped up on a pillow. The southerner, Jamie, was filming us while eating candy. They were having a grand old time. They wanted to continue straight through, but we were set steadfastly against it.

"Mate, who cares? Let's go on through."

"Dude, it's the checkpoint. It's not the right way."

Our disagreement became a raging argument. If it were the entrance to Fallujah, I thought, they would have gone in all the same. Stopped in the middle of the road, in the middle of the night, just outside a checkpoint, we were beginning to attract attention.

Crabb finally had enough. "I'm shitting my pants, mate! I'm not fucking going through that way. No chance!"

This made the other Aussies laugh and tipped the scale in our favor. We recommenced our awkward reverse back toward the roundabout, where we found a furtive right-hand turn. Both cars proceeded uphill until running into a small village. This, we quickly ascertained, was not the correct direction either. At wit's end, I flagged a car going downhill with three teens inside. They spoke little English and only a bit of Hebrew.

"*Ivrit?*" (Hebrew?)

"No."

"*Aravit?*" (Arabic?)

"No."

"*Anglit?*"

"Yes. English."

The boys then looked at each other, muttered something suspicious in Arabic, and looked back at us. We were disrupting the quiet night. Dogs began to bark around us, piercing the silence of the village. One of the young Arab boys got out of the car and began to approach.

Crabb got nervous. "No, mate. No good. Go-go-go."

Jeff fired up the engine as the boy drew near, pulling away at a rapid clip. Suddenly, a giant camel materialized from the night, tethered to a rope on the side of the road. Jeff slammed on the brakes, and we lurched forward, too startled to mutter a word. The four of us looked at each other in surreal disbelief as the massive, equally alarmed camel straddled the embankment, kicking, spitting, hissing. What the *hell* was going on? We needed to get out of there, quick.

Back down the hill, there was no place to turn around, and it was impossible to reverse past the roundabout, through the tunnel. Running out of options, Jeff decided to jump the tiny rental car over a cement median. After a thorough grating of the undercarriage we sped up the road in the other direction. Looking back through the side-view mirror, the soldiers did not seem to pay us any mind. I wondered if they had noticed us at all. And I could not get that cursed camel out of my head.

Back in Jerusalem, we stumbled into a hotel to regroup and ask for advice. With a rather quizzical expression, a friendly concierge informed us that, one, we were going the right direction; two, the purported checkpoint was only a barrier; and three, although Road 1 cut through the West Bank, it was a secure Israeli-only road. After being sufficiently upbraided by the meatheads in car number two, we set off (again) for the Dead Sea. But it was now nearly five o'clock, and getting to the top of Masada in time for sunrise grew less probable by the minute.

In the lightening predawn sky, passing through the barrier was no more trouble than taking Fastrak across the Golden Gate Bridge: we sped right through. The daybreak drive was peaceful, serene.

Reflecting on the recent fiasco, I realized that, ironically, the darkness had shed light on my perceptions of the West Bank. It illuminated that as much as I wanted to experience a peaceful reality in Palestine, part of me suspected much worse. My mind filled the void beyond the checkpoint with images of faceless Arabs out to get us. They were mean and scary; they were everywhere. The dispersonified other, by nature of his otherness, somehow became less than human. Though I did not know it at the time, the idea of tacitly including one's preconceived notions in their experience of reality would reveal itself in a profound way just several weeks later, when I entered the West Bank on an entirely different type of journey.

When we finally arrived, the sun hung low over the bleached hills of Jordan to the east. We had missed sunrise, but the large rocky outcropping of Masada stood proud and defiant, a giant geological fist uppercutting the barren landscape below. The only way up its front face was a rugged switchback trail. In the back a giant mechanical tram sloped toward a lowered plateau. Ascent from that side was only possible, for a time, via another snake path.

As our crew began to hike the face, we teased and bantered excitedly. Wiggy chugged lemonade from the nearby concession stand, and Bennett lit a smoke, blaring music through speakers in his backpack. We threw stones at Rees and Thew marching in advance. But as the trek became more demanding, chatter receded, eyes focused on the rocky steps ahead, the huff-puffing of out-of-shape baseball players growing audible. I thought of a story I had been told on Birthright in this very location several years prior. In reality, most of what is known about the event comes from the Roman historian Josephus.

Around the year 66 CE, Masada was home to a Jewish community, the Zealots. Fleeing Roman persecution, they established an emergency hideaway in this most inhospitable of locations, overlooking the Dead Sea. After so many days it was necessary to walk north to the natural springs of Ein Gedi in order to retrieve fresh water, lugging it back to man-made wells. On top of Masada a synagogue was built, along with a library, a royal residence, and, of course, heavy artillery stockpiles and fortifications. Given the acute slope of both entrances and the hideaway's strategic elevated location, the Israelites were able to hold off attacking forces for many months. Eventually, the Romans built a large ramp from the rear, up which to charge soldiers and roll a Goliath catapult. The night before the Romans were to launch a full-scale attack, the Jewish community on Masada decided to take action rather than face sure defeat. In a macabre and somewhat controversial final act, the community of more than nine hundred committed mass suicide: the men killed the women and children and then each other, the last of whom took his own life. Some thought this was cowardly, reflecting poorly on the Jewish people, while some believed it was an honorable if tragic deed in the face of a dominant oppressor. Others believed the story a mere myth. I reserved judgment.

An hour later our crew reached the top, shirts drenched in sweat. Since I pitched the day before, even though I'd done so terribly, I figured I'd use the hike as my daily cardio, keeping a decent pace. Only Rees was quicker. At the top I caught my breath and turned around to see everyone following behind, except for Johnny Thew. He was far down the path, hands on his head, slugging water. He would join us twenty minutes later, announcing his arrival in vomit. Though it would have been nice to witness the sunrise again, the experience was no less powerful. After taking pictures, each went his own way to explore. I sent a quick text to Yael, telling her I was not dead, then walked over to view the intimidating Roman ramp.

Several rooms back I wandered into the remnants of a shul. There was a modern mezuzah fastened to the entrance, a display of ancient pottery with Hebrew writing. I thought back several weeks earlier to the café in Tel Aviv where Rothem had taught me the Hebrew alphabet. He typed letters on his Smartphone, and we spent the afternoon eating watermelon while going over the vaguely familiar symbols, myself the student and Rothem the teacher. "*Alef, bet, gimel . . . alef, bet, gimel,*" I intoned, over and over and over.

Sitting in the shul, it occurred to me that people had been speaking this language for thousands of years. From scrolls to text messages the Hebrew language had endured, survived. This reinforced in me the importance of keeping the roots, of preserving a beautiful tradition that deserved to live on, in spite of so many forces—Roman, Nazi, and so on—attempting to stand in the way.

As I sat in quiet contemplation on the ancient stone bench inside the temple, a renewed realization that Jews had been living in this land for millennia welled proudly inside. I felt connected to the history, to everything around me. I was not a half-Jew, and certainly not a half-assed Jew, bar mitzvah or no bar mitzvah. Let the ticket lady slap a "5" on my bag now, I thought. As often as I disagreed with Israeli actions in the back-and-forth of the conflict, Masada made clear that Jews had a patent claim to this land. But then again, so did Palestinians. It was their land too; they had been here for hundreds of years. Acceptance of one truth, I thought, might not simultaneously exclude another. Perhaps it had never been a black-and-white, right-or-wrong zero-sum game.

Rising from my seat, I grabbed a stone from the floor and tossed it off the edge toward the Roman ramp below, watching it fall, fall. Then I felt something sting me in the back. I had just been plucked.

"Oy, mate. That's a sissy toss. Have one right here in me chest."

"Oh yeah?" I responded playfully to Wigg. "Come here. I'll toss *you* off just like I did that rock."

"You wouldn't do that, now, would you, mate? Who's gonna catch you in the All-Star Game tomorrow if I go sailing off that cliff?"

"Good point," I answered back.

Leaving Masada, we headed for the Dead Sea. We floated in supersaturated salty water that stung the eyes, burned stray cuts. We took mud baths at the Ein Gedi resort, submerged beneath odorous sulfur pools, napped in the grass under shady palms. As I lay there, I had completely forgotten about the previous day's loss. That night's adventures, too, had seemed foreign, dream-like. With my head in the grass and my mind in the sky, starting the All-Star Game was far from my thoughts, a world away. And there was no way—no way—that camel had been real.

24 All-Star Game

"CHA-CHA-CHA, CHA-CHA, CHA-CHA-CHA, CHA-CHA."
As the doors of the bus opened several hours before the All-Star Game at Yarkon, we were greeted by a mass of horns passionately overlaying a traditional Latin rhythm. The mood was unapologetically festive. De Los Santos, a.k.a. Matacaballo, the übercharismatic shortstop for Netanya, had thrown a mix into the PA, and the Dominicans were grooving jovially. Approaching the field we witnessed Crabbie pop out of the dugout, kicking his rugby football into right field in the traditional short-hop style. Rees, Thew, and Wigg ran after it, tackling each other and rolling around like so many dingoes.

After a little horseplay, it was time for the home run derby. The announcer garbled that for each hitter Round 1 would consist of five outs each, anything that wasn't a bomb. Josh Doane, the center fielder for Netanya, hit first, followed by Petach Tikva's Ryan Crotin, Modi'in's Eladio Rodriguez, Bet Shemesh's Johnny Lopez, Ra'anana's Juan Ramirez, and Tel Aviv's very own Stuart

"Pupo" Brito. In a lackluster and somewhat embarrassing effort, nobody took one deep. Not a promising start for the IBL's very first All-Star Game.

Round 2, however, got things going. Someone threw on an MTV *Jock Jams* CD, which riled the modest turnout of fans, and the players responded. Each went yard, while Crotin and Pupo blasted three apiece, vaulting a Jew and a Dominican into the finals.

People began streaming into the stadium as the final round commenced. Crotin was up first, on his second swing blasting a line drive just over the fence in left. But this would be his only home run. Pupo then strolled to the plate. The seven other Lightning All-Stars—Fish, Jeff, Frankie, Langbord, Rothem, Wigg, and I—plus all the Dominicans, started to cheer from the outfield where we were shagging. Brito needed two dingers to win it. He flexed through his faded blue Under Armour T, turned his hat around, and dug in. But for all the show, he recorded three consecutive outs. Just two remaining. On the fourth pitch he launched a towering blast to left, nearly hitting the Baptist Village apartments beyond the fence. His next swing sent the pitch just as far, but straight up, landing after an eternity in front of the pitcher's mound.

With an out remaining the score was tied at one home run each. Pupo stepped out of the box, shrugged his shoulders, and cracked his neck. He stepped back in, scraped his right foot deep into the dirt, raised his bat toward Skip throwing BP. Skip grooved one, but Pupo let it go. *Jock Jams* still pumping, the crowd grew louder. We yelled more fervently from left field. Pupo took a deep breath, raised his bat once again, said, "*Okay,*" and nodded toward the mound. On the next pitch he swung hard, the ball exiting his bat with a crisp crack, on a trajectory somewhere between the prior out and his last home run. The rainbow fly apexed high above left-center field, approaching the fence on its decline. Matacaballo glided back with a huge grin, mitt extended toward the sky. He reached the wall and, hoping to rob Pupo, pressed against it. But the ball landed several feet beyond his grasp.

At that moment the Dominican entourage sprinted in from the outfield to congratulate Pupo at home. They were hopping up and down in a circle, slapping Brito on his head, yelling, "*Dominica, Dominica*, yeeeeeeeee!" Their spirit lifted the energy of the entire stadium. As they settled down, Johnny Fogerty replaced *Jock Jams*, and the crowd nodded to "Put Me in, Coach" as everyone prepared for the game.

Each player was wearing his team jersey. Our side, the South, wore a white mesh IBL All-Star Game hat with blue lettering. The North's colors were inverted. Initially, our box of lids was placed on the helmet rack in the dugout. Wiggy ran over, took five, shoved them in his bag. When there were not enough to go around he surreptitiously returned three to the box on the rack. "Oy, mate, have a look," he said. "There's a couple caps right hea."

As we were trying them on, Skip ambled over with his distinctive wry grin. "How are ya, Aaron?"

"What's up, Skip? Nice BP you were throwing to Pupo. I think his victory was all you."

"I just throw 'em down the middle."

"That's right."

After adequate small talk, Skip revealed his true motive for approaching me. "So, you deserve to be starting this game. You've thrown great all season, and you earned the start, no doubt about it."

"Thanks. I appreciate that."

"But I'm not gonna throw you. You just pitched two days ago, and it doesn't make sense running you out there again." After a pause he added, "But I want to win this thing. If it's close at the end, we may use you."

"Okay. You got it," I replied.

"All right, then, here we go."

The pregame pageantry was slightly less explosive than the first inning we put on the North. Hastings led off with a vicious double to right-center. The next two hitters singled and fouled out, respectively. Then Fish, who was hitting cleanup, knocked in Jeff for our first run. By the time we were through, their starter was out, Maximo was in, and we were up 5–zilch.

The North, however, would respond. Rees hit a massive three-run bomb in the third, which actually hit the Village apartments in left. In the fourth Eladio singled in a run and Matt Bennett doubled in another to tie the game at 5–5. It would remain tied until the top of the eighth, as pitchers from both sides settled in and threw well, including a one-two-three fifth from Rothem, the only Israeli All-Star from either side.

In the middle of the sixth the announcer said, "At this point we would like to extend a warm thank-you to Larry Baras. If it wasn't for his vision, this league truly would never have existed."

He was right. It gave people the warm fuzzies; fans crooned with applause. In the dugout, however, Crabb quipped, "Yeah? Where's my fucking money? It's two weeks late!"

This seemed a precise encapsulation of the league and our experience. On the outside all was seamless and smooth. It was a league with no problems, and everything worked. Fans cheered; games were on TV. But the emperor had no clothes. On the inside people were yelling and screaming, and no one had any answers. Yet another mutually inclusive contradiction of this league, this country.

Between the seventh and eighth innings, a friendly reporter from our previously televised games asked if she could do an in-game interview with me and some of the other players. She said to make it fun, that we should be playful. Of course, I obliged.

We were huddled in the dugout. "Are you enjoying your experience so far?" She stuck the mic in my face, a bright light from the camera shining just over her shoulder.

"Yes, it's been great. I'm really enjoying my time. I think baseball in Israel is sort of a grand experiment. Judging by the turnout tonight I'd say we're doing okay."

"And how does the level of play here compare to other professional leagues in America?"

"I think there's a slight talent gap in this league. There are some truly seasoned professionals and some younger guys right out of college, so it's a nice mix. But I'll tell you, seeing all the best players competing on the same field at the same time tonight really highlights the IBL's tremendous upside. I think the composition of players in this All-Star Game is as good as any league I've been a part of back in the States."

I spread an optimistic gloss over a sentiment I'd echoed at other times more vindictively, but one needed to stay positive on TV.

After volleying several boilerplate questions, it was time to turn on the charm. Grabbing the mic from the reporter, I began interviewing Rothem sitting next to me. She had, after all, said to have a little fun. "So Dan . . . ," I said to Rothem's surprise and discomfort, "as the only Israeli to make the All-Star team, after having one of the only one-two-three innings of the night, do you feel a sense of pride, a sense of bringing glory to your country?"

He gave a shy chuckle and then a diplomatic response to the camera in Hebrew. It was a kick in the shorts; I enjoyed embarrassing him.

Just then Pupo, who won the home run derby several hours earlier, walked by, and I interviewed him in Spanish while translating for the viewers at home. "Pupo, *como te sientes sobre ganando el* home run derby? *Como estaba?*"

"*Bien,*" he said. "*Esperé un buen pitch y traté de hacer contacto.*"

Looking into the camera I declared, "Well, Mr. Brito just told us that he waited for a good pitch and tried to make contact." He too knew his clichés. I hoped the reporter and the viewers at home were entertained.

In the top of the eighth (the All-Star Game was extended to nine innings), Johnny Lopez knocked in Eladio to put the North up 6–5. With the game previously tied, I figured there was a strong chance I'd throw the ninth. But since the North took the lead, if we did not score a run here or the following inning we wouldn't need another pitcher; the game would be over. On the other hand, if we came back to tie it in the ninth, there would be an even better chance that I'd close out the tenth. I knew Skip had confidence in me, that he wanted to win. Trying to focus, it was difficult to ignore the "pitching probability barometer" implanted in every reliever's head.

Between the eighth and ninth innings, still down one run, Skip left the front of the dugout and began walking toward me, his eyes revealing what he wanted to say. He was going to tell me to throw the next inning, should we tie it up. "How do you feel?"

"Good." I thought he was referring to my arm.

"Okay. Go get loose." He flipped his right fist outward, the universal sign for swing. "Grab a bat." My stomach shifted from a feeling of angst to excitement, sensing the significance of the moment. I headed down the right-field line for some warmup hacks, envisioning winning the first-ever All-Star Game on a walk-off home run. Though I began hitting several weeks into the season, having done so in college as well, this would be my biggest at bat of the year. That is, if I got the call.

In the bottom of the ninth the first hitter grounded out. Then on a 3-1 count, the second hitter drew a walk. A home run by the next batter would end the game. From the third base coach's box, Skip put his left fist on top of his right, wiggling them back and forth in a Barry Bonds–like twitch, signaling for a pinch hitter. I walked in from the right-field line to grab a helmet.

Fish was standing close by. "You're up."

"Yep."

I gave him a mischievous squint of the eyes. Crossing paths with Wigg, whom I had just replaced, we exchanged fist bumps.

Walking to the plate I was excited, not nervous. This season I had hit or played first in about half our games. Pitching I probably took too seriously, but hitting was pure exhilarating fun. This was my chance to be the hero, every boy's playground fantasy. On the hill was Feliciano, Bet Shemesh's ace and the league's best pitcher. In our last encounter he beat me with a slider low and in, sufficiently off-speed to induce a pop fly to right, just short of the close fence at Gezer.

Before digging in I took a practice swing and noted the situation. One out, one on, down a run. I could tell Feliciano was pumped. A true professional, this was the type of environment in which he thrived: fans cheering, great pressure. The first pitch was a fastball middle-out. Feliciano was throwing from the stretch with a runner on first, and his slide-step delivery was quicker than I'd expected. I took a huge hack. The force of overswinging shifted my weight back, causing me to hop several times on my left leg, which was better than falling over. As I finished the swing, my head shot up instinctively, staring out toward the right-field fence in the direction I expected the ball to be traveling. But I had swung over the top, several moments late. There was a loud POP in Eladio's glove behind me. Head on the ball, I thought. Stepping out of the box, I looked at Skip as he went through the signs . . . nothing on.

As Feliciano began his motion once again, the runner on first broke for second, which was confusing since Skip did not give the steal. The pitch was down Main Street, but since the runner had caught my attention I couldn't pull the trigger. Eladio swiftly exchanged the ball from his catcher's glove to his throwing hand, firing a laser to second, throwing the vacuous runner out by several steps. It was a big play for the North, and they were pumped, their fans cheering eagerly. I understood the runner was trying to get into scoring position down 6–5, but with Feliciano's quick delivery and Eladio's rifle behind the dish, it was not a smart time to steal. And with a lefty up, odds were favorable that he would advance on a grounder or sac fly to the right side, putting him in scoring position anyway. Further, there were now two outs instead of one, and with nobody on we could no longer win the game on a single swing.

Shifting from the stretch to the windup, energized to be out of a small jam, Feliciano squared his body and looked directly at me. He raised his glove, flicking it in a straight line toward home—the universal sign for fastball. It was a loaded gesture; he did not have to say a word. Feliciano had challenged me, loud, in public, for all to see. His simple wave of the glove said, "Okay, me and you. I know you can't beat me. In fact, I'm so sure of it I'll tell you what's coming. I've thrown you two fastballs already, and I'm gonna give you another. Let's see what you got, homeboy." I did not know whether to be offended or inspired, and to be honest, I didn't care, just wanted to go deep. Players from both sides had observed the gesture, and the two dugouts howled impatiently. *Come on. Let's go*, I said to myself.

Feliciano was ready. He stepped back with his left leg, swung it tightly against his chest, releasing a fastball. It reached me instantly, at the last second tailing sharply away with a little sink for good measure. The first pitch I had had a good shot at, the second who knows. This pitch, without the slightest bit of hyperbole, was the best I had ever seen (after the game I was told the three pitches were 89, 91, and 93 miles per hour, respectively). I knew I could not hit a 93-mph fastball low and away with sharp, late sink. But I swung hard, aiming for the location at which I expected the ball to arrive. It was several inches off my bat, already several moments behind me. I wasn't close.

Walking back to the dugout, I removed my helmet and batting gloves, while the North sprinted onto the field to celebrate their victory in the first-ever IBL All-Star Game.

SECOND HALF

25 Progress Report; or, Every Five Days

An embarrassed Israeli military confirmed Sunday that a soldier from an elite brigade was left behind by his comrades in the Gaza Strip last week, and that he was extricated only after they had returned to base.

New York Times, July 29, 2007

AFTER SEVERAL DAYS' BREAK WE WERE READY TO launch into the second half of the season. Since the league was a mere two months long, everyone's attention turned toward finishing strong for playoffs, just weeks away. Before doing so, however, it seemed appropriate to reflect on the season thus far, in order to make adjustments both personal and leaguewide as we moved into the home stretch.

If I were the IBL's teacher, I mused, I would have called home a long time ago. It's an effective strategy to employ around the first third of the semester, in order to preempt any parental concerns that may arise from the first progress report. In my talks with Kurtzer and Baras during the initial meetings, as well as subsequent informal chats around the diamond, I thought I'd accomplished the equivalent of calling home to the league's mom and dad. It was now time for the progress report, the midterm grades. Though the evaluation would not be included in any official transcripts or judgments, an update seemed necessary in order to chart the best path for the second half of the season. And if no one cared to listen to a washed-up former pro, if that label could be used at all, such ruminations at least ameliorated my instinctual need to evaluate and assess. I got out the red pen. Instead of English, history, math, and science, the league would be graded on communication, organization, homework, and, of course, chutzpah.

Communication had thus far been the single biggest problem (that and a lack of fields, fans, and equipment). Many of the debacles surrounding payment, gym memberships, ice, trainers, buses, and food could have been quelled with a more regular, accurate, coherent transfer of information. Or at least more regular and accurate. Or at least more regular. Players really just wanted to think they knew what was transpiring. Complaining most likely would not have decreased, but at least it would have been less justified. Put a whiteboard in the cafeteria with announcements. Create a phone tree. Send a group e-mail. Communication by word of mouth was failing. F.

Organization was also a huge clusterfuck. To the league's credit, things had gotten better, but barely. The IBL was functioning at a minimum threshold, which is to say it had not completely fallen apart. Belatedly, players had shekels and dollars instead of uncashable checks. Guys had a place to sleep, but there was no rhyme or reason as to room assignments. And there was a mishmash schedule rather than one arranged by series, in which pitchers regularly threw against the same teams, games were canceled, and more than once several teams had played *two* doubleheaders in *one* week with *eight* pitchers. Then there was the lack of bats and balls. It would turn out that much of the auxiliary equipment was held up in customs, but, like my dog ate my homework, this was no excuse. Or maybe it was. Late was acceptable, but just barely. The league was passing in organization, but it would need to do some work over the summer. D-minus.

To the league's credit, it had done its homework. Much of the back-end preparation, like having tryouts and a draft, printing tickets, getting investors and advertising, creating team names and uniforms, and putting together a Web site, had been accomplished deftly and with time to spare. In fact, Baras mentioned that 95 percent of the details were completed beforehand but the last 5 percent were giving him fits. By this calculation he'd probably give the league an A. From a player's perspective, I'd say they were proficient. B.

To attempt to establish a baseball league in the Middle East, for real, took an incredible amount of chutzpah. That Baras and the gang mostly pulled it off was incredible and worthy of high praise. Playing America's pastime in the Holy Land was a tremendous if quixotic idea of which I was proud to be a part. When Larry said he put together the league for the benefit of the people of Israel, to bring joy to the lives of families, to teach them this beautiful game, I believed him. He and his crew deserved a ton of credit. In the chutzpah column, the IBL scored an A-plus.

But the devil was in the details, and in the details improvement was needed. With several weeks to go it was unclear whether the league was limping or sprinting to the finish line. We'd have to wait until then, to see how the final grades would come out. Those marks would count for real, and one could never make up their freshman year. Well, I supposed one could—I'd seen it before—but to repeat was downright embarrassing.

If the league was barely passing, the Tel Aviv Lightning was doing better than average. We had seventeen wins and eight losses, plus two ties (but we'll get to those later). Modi'in had fallen one game behind us, while we were trailing the Mighty Blue Sox by two. Jeff, Fish, Brito, Frankie, and the rest of the gang were still hitting well, though not with the electric intensity of the first few weeks. And our pitching remained solid, though some arms were showing signs of fatigue, a little wear and tear.

Finally, I had to look in the mirror: was I limping or sprinting to the finish line? I'd doled out plenty of criticism to the league, and it was only fair to look inward. Skip decided I'd forgo pitching in the All-Star Game in order to begin fresh the second half of the season. Perhaps not throwing even an inning was pusillanimous. But this was the home stretch, and I wanted to put our chances of winning ahead of everything else. How was I throwing? I asked myself. I knew I was five and two, near the top of the league in wins, even though I'd lost my last two games. My ERA? No idea. Didn't want to know. Part of the whole PROCESS OVER PRODUCT thing.

To be honest, I was relatively pleased with my performance. The break, including the All-Star Game and our escapade through Ramallah to the Dead Sea, helped enable me to reconcile the last Modi'in loss, to flush it, forget about it. And incredibly, gone were the initial arm troubles that raised doubts about my ability to pitch at all. For this alone, I was grateful. *Diyenu.*

Sitting in quiet contemplation outside my room at the *kfar* in the (not so) early morning sun, I found myself rubbing my elbow absentmindedly. What day was it? I thought frantically. My heart began to beat; my ears became warm. I had forgotten the day of my next start. Trouble. I counted backward. I threw against Modi'in last Friday. Saturday. Yesterday, Sunday, was the All-Star Game. Today was Monday. Saturday, Sunday, Monday was three, so I'd throw again Tuesday . . . Wednesday. I breathed a sigh of relief, still two more days. And that, I realized, had become my life.

Most people begin the workweek on Monday. They aim for Wednesday—hump day—sliding into Friday afternoon. Two all too quick days of rest, then back on it. A seven-day loop. Five on, two off, and so forth, for as long as it takes.

But to be a starting pitcher, it seemed, was to lead a markedly different existence. And at the center of this universe lies Start Day. It makes the rest of the world light or dark, warm or cold. It's the fuel, the eternal force around which all other days rotate.

That night, in victory or defeat, in happiness or sorrow, you tipple aplenty. The following day you go for a protracted run, sweating out equal portions alcohol and lactic acid. Depending on how the wing is feeling you may or may not have a light catch. The second day, in order to stretch it out, you throw as far as 120–50 feet. By this point you hope the arm is not sore but tight, and a long easy toss will do it good. Afterward you run more distance but also mix in something explosive. Maybe you run poles and do a jog-sprint-jog, or some amalgamation thereof. Day 3 is more of the same, but you throw with a bit more effort, sprinkling in a few change-ups and sliders as you walk it in from longtoss. Running this day is another aerobic-anaerobic combination, leaning more heavily toward the latter. Maybe ten poles and eight sprints. The fourth day you throw up to ninety feet, the length of a base path, ending with a short, flat bullpen to keep your touch on all three pitches. You either run a few sprints or do nothing at all, in order to rest your legs, because Start Day is approaching.

During this time you're also mixing in some weights. But if your elbow has recently had issues you don't want to risk reaggravation, though you continue your Jobe's religiously. You're also doing sit-ups like a ninja, icing and self-medicating as needed.

Gastronomically, there are two major rules. One: drink a surfeit of water the day before a start in order to hydrate, knowing you sweat profusely. Two: no eating at the *kfar* on Start Day—period. Instead, wake up early, grab two *rugelach* (rolled Jewish pastries) and a drinkable yogurt from Guy's Place alongside the gas station across the street. Also pick up a sandwich and some crappy Israeli energy bars to stuff in your bag since there is no food at the field. Eat the first half of the sandwich before you get on the bus and the second in the dugout ninety minutes before the game. Then change from shorts and shoes into your uniform. Since it takes forty-five minutes to get ready, you have fifteen minutes to chill. Try not to sweat prematurely in the desert heat. If you're the home team you go out forty-five minutes before;

if you're away go five to ten minutes after that. You're wearing pants and cleats at this point, but no jersey. That you'll put on in the bullpen.

It's time to begin. You walk to the outfield, taking along a sweat rag and timepiece. You run two poles to get loose, then stretch arms and legs. This takes about fifteen minutes. After walking back to the dugout you grab your jersey, your glove, and a pearl, head back down the line, and begin throwing with the backup catcher, since Wiggy is taking infield-outfield. You back up to 120 feet, stretching it out lightly. You check your watch: thirty minutes have passed. As you walk in you start throwing harder, making sure to stay on top of the baseball, no arc, keeping it flat. When you get to 50 feet you mix in a few changes and sliders, then throw two- and four-seam fastballs until reaching the line. Then you jump on the bullpen mound, where Wiggy is waiting, and get half warmed up from the stretch. Two fastballs away, two in, two more away, two more in, three changes, three sliders, two more fastballs. Then you step back, take thirty seconds to wipe the sweat from your arms and face, and take a deep breath. You check your watch: ten minutes until game time. From the windup you repeat the same sequence, adding a variety of randomly selected pitches, ending with several final fastballs. It has taken about forty-two minutes, and you walk in with three to spare. You get a sip of water, sit down, and wait to begin. You're ready. This is the fifth day, Start Day. It's go time.

You pitch.

You tipple.

You wake up and repeat the same five-day sequence all over again. And again and again for as long as it takes.

26 Fourth Time's a Charm

Before I knew it, Start Day had arrived once again. While I'd been granted a two-game reprieve from the Mighty Blue Sox, I was currently on a personal two-game skid. Though Bet Shemesh was still in first, for all my bickering before our previous encounter this was perhaps just what I needed to get back on track. Because I desperately needed to get back on track.

My fourth start versus the Blue Sox in eight appearances, a win would put us just one game out of first. Though currently 3-0 in head-to-head match-ups, it was not getting any easier. Plus, this was our first bout at the unpredictable Kibbutz Gezer. After coming off my worst outing of the season I wanted to throw well, but also did not want to press. Just keep the same approach: process over product.

Heading into the last inning we had scored only two runs the entire game, stranding runners on several occasions. On the bright side, I was jogging to the mound with a two-run lead. I had had an extra day's rest because of the All-Star break (every six days), and I think this helped my stuff. Against Bet Shemesh, however, and especially at the Geez, good stuff was not always enough. Up to this point in the season my slider had not been that effective. So I worked between starts on throwing it better, which is to say with a sharper break and a location that stays in the strike zone longer, either the whole time or dipping just out of the zone for the last ten to fifteen feet after the hitter has already committed his swing. In addition, after throwing against the Blue Sox three times, they had seen plenty of my fastball and change, so featuring the breaking ball more significantly would be a nice way to mix rhythm, keep hitters on their toes.

In the bottom of the seventh I picked up the baseball, which had rolled down the back slope of the mound onto the infield grass, cupping it in my hands. I was rubbing it up when the horizon caught my eye. The days were getting shorter, and even though this had been a quick game, the sky seemed much darker than usual for this time of day. The softball lights had just come on. Looking out past first base I noticed the sunset. I didn't expect it to come so soon, and it caught me by surprise. In spite of my current task I stole a moment, drank it in. Off to the west a stout light pole dissected the outer third of the giant glowing sun, while a bushy tree on the outskirts of the yard encroached from underneath upon its belly. As the sun set over the valley below, its light painted the western sky in reds, yellows, and oranges. I turned and looked left past the raised plateau of Kibbutz Gezer, beyond the sunflower fields, toward the tomb of Solomon, former ruler of the Kingdom of Israel. Just above the ridge a sliver of light-blue sky was surrendering to a thick slab of twilight, which in turn yielded to the star-speckled blackness of the heavens above. I made a final scan from left to right of the multicolored horizon before turning toward home, in the process chuckling at having absorbed such superfluous detail in this critical moment. For some reason, it relaxed me.

I looked at the dusty rubber beneath my feet, focusing my thoughts with a slow, deep inhale and a quick breath out. Okay, let's do it. Looking up I found Wigg settling into his crouch. After the last warmup pitch, as Wiggy threw down to second, I stepped off the right side of the mound and waited to receive the ball from Fish, the final stop on its way around the horn.

"Come on, *Preeeeb*," he said and flipped me the ball, his long hair dangling from beneath his hat. Three, four, five were coming up, the heart of their order save Raymundo, whom I struck out to end the sixth with the ninth batter on first. He was on base only because the ump demonstratively tacked ball three onto a 2-1 count for licking my fingers while standing on the side of the mound. Seriously. In my first start of the year I asked another ump about this very rule, and he said the dirt was okay, just not the rubber. But this guy wanted to let everyone know he was in control, so he called ball three without even so much as a professional courteous warning.

Skip came rushing out of the dugout waving a finger at the ump. "What? Hey! Whoa?! No-no-no. What?"

In hindsight we would fear for Skip's health. Debacles such as this, of which there were many, had begun to take their toll on the old sage.

In short order Skip realized any appeal to logic, reason, or civility was useless. He turned around, steaming, and walked back to the dugout, only to turn back toward the ump once again. "Hold on. You mean to tell me that in the sixth inning of a close game you're gonna pull some shit like this? How . . . who in their . . . " Fire spat from Skip's ears. He flapped his hand at the ump and spun back toward the dugout before the ump could get in a word.

With Skip safely in the dugout, I managed to fill the count but walked the ninth hitter on a fastball down. This wasn't an excuse to walk the guy, but, yes, the umpire was a sack of rusty nickels. Fortunately, I struck out the next hitter, the leadoff, on a hard slider down. When Raymundo came up with a runner on first, representing the tying run, it was a precarious situation. This time with the help of Rusty Nickels, intentionally or otherwise, I caught Raymundo on a called strike-three change-up several inches off the plate. Clearly, it was a ball, but I walked off the mound like it was a strike all along.

Back in the bottom of the seventh, with King Solomon watching posthumously from left in the twilight tableau, I straddled the rubber, set to begin. The league's home run leader, Jason Rees, was leading off. In the dugout between innings, Wigg and I talked about how we would approach him. We knew he'd roll over a good fastball low and away. In fact, we tried this his first time up. But I threw a fastball down the dick, and he crushed it, though I was somehow able to stab the sharp liner hit back up the box. The next time we got him on a first-pitch change-up. Here in the seventh, we decided to lead with another change. It missed low and away, and since it did not remain in the zone for long enough, Rees didn't bite. The next pitch I threw an outside fastball. As we discussed in the dugout, he rolled it over, grounding to Fish, who threw him out. Phew. The first one was always huge.

The next batter was Johnny Lopez. He skied a 1-1 hanging slider miles into the firmament. Langbord raced back, ball still climbing, and camped just short of the hill in center. He waited. Eventually, the ball came down, landing in Langer's mitt. The pitch was off-speed just enough to get Lopez out in front, turning a would-be dinger into a pop fly. Two outs.

I received the ball from Fish once again and stepped back up the mound. Bet Shemesh consistently drew the most fans, and Lopez's near miss brought their febrile cheering to a climax. Feeling the adrenaline, the momentum, I was three strikes away from snapping a two-game losing streak. And, more important, we were on the verge of clawing back to within a game of first place. The Blue Sox may have had the fans on their side, but King Solomon and the sunflowers were on mine.

Next up was Bet Shemesh's catcher, the guy Langbord trucked at home plate during our second match-up, nearly causing a brawl. I thought back to Skip's words that day: "Not now. Maybe in a few weeks when he's not expecting it." But this wasn't the time to hit him; the game was too close. Instead, I humped up for a first-pitch fastball. It got way too much of the plate, but luckily he swung right through. He abstained from the second pitch, a middle-in slider that stayed in the zone just long enough for Wigg, extending his glove as far as possible, to catch at the knees. Strike two. I stepped off the rubber for a brief second, looked down, took a deep breath. Two outs, two strikes, up two runs, on the precipice of an important victory.

Returning to the rubber, I looked in for the sign. Wigg put down his pointer finger and then turned over his hand palm out, flapping his fingers against it, motioning for me to throw the ball high above the zone. He wanted to ladder him, to see if their catcher would climb up and chase a deliberately elevated pitch. I nodded, wound up, delivered. He swung, fouling it over the short chain-link backstop. A little higher and we might have gotten him, I thought, but the pitch was at his letters instead of up in his eyes. Still 0–2.

This time Wigg wiggled four fingers, calling for a change. I shook. He called for a fastball away. I shook again. He finally put down three fingers, the pitch I was looking for, and I began my windup before so much as nodding in recognition. It was sharp, like I worked on days prior, and as the slider dipped down out of the strike zone their catcher swung over the top for strike three.

Stalking off the mound toward our dugout, I chucked my glove at the bottom of the fence. I felt relieved and oddly upset, pissed at having to throw against Bet Shemesh for a fourth time, not knowing how to possibly do so again.

It was a big win and the fire, welling up inside, spilled out. "Yeeeeeeeeah!" I shouted. "*Fuck* yeah!"

The team rushed from our dugout and began swatting my head, knocking off my hat. After a few moments of jubilation, I grabbed my lid from the ground and walked down the left-field line for our postgame chat, toward the sunflowers and King Solomon's tomb.

27 The Clara Fashion Bar

AFTER MY FOURTH START AGAINST BET SHEMESH I was spent, both physically and emotionally. Not throwing for another five days, I went out on the town, let loose a bit. Some of the younger players in the league partied nearly every night, but I preferred to pick my spots. And after a start was always a good bet.

I was still talking to Yael. In fact, I saw her most often in the evening after games. I had discovered, however, that she preferred to spend time with me alone, rather than with the guys. That night when I told her what we were up to she said she couldn't make it. Detecting a hint of petulance in her voice, I brushed it off, blamed it on her prickly sabra disposition: tough on the outside, sweet within.

With Yael on the sidelines, I tried to round up a crew. Fish was in his room painting and spinning records, lost in a world of his own. One could not mess with moments of artistic expression such as this, and I did not want to break his dervishlike focus. Fish was out. Hastings, usually down for anything, called it an early night, adding veracity to the thirty-seven-year-old's moniker, Old Man River. Jeff was out, too. That left me, the Arch Conservative Levy, Wigg, and a guy from Bet Shemesh who had moved to Israel from New York several years earlier. I didn't know Mike, a backup catcher, was on their team until he piled into a cab with us outside the *kfar*.

We entered Tel Aviv several minutes later, heading south on Ben Yehuda, one block removed from the water. Because of the street name we talked about languages, about how Hebrew is ancient yet in some ways very young. And by "we" I mean everyone but Wiggy, who was hopped up on Red Bull and ready to party.

The three of us discussed the fact that Hebrew had been spoken for millennia, since biblical times, but "died" in the 500s because of Jewish persecution. From then on it remained in use for liturgical purposes, but people stopped speaking it in the vernacular. Hebrew would remain this way for another fourteen hundred years. In the 1880s, when Israel was still part of Palestine in the Ottoman Empire, a man named Ben Yehuda moved to the desert with his wife and son. He permitted only Hebrew to be spoken in the home, which was difficult, considering words for things like the telephone, car, and fastball did not exist. So they made up a few, borrowing here and there from other sources, breathing life into the ancient dialect, resurrecting an avatar of the holy tongue. Coinciding with Ben Yehuda's death in 1922, several years after Britain took over Palestine as a mandate following World War I, Hebrew, English, and Arabic became the territory's three official languages. When Israel gained statehood in 1948, after a debate about its proper location in which some suggested southern Africa and others South America, there was also a debate about the official language of the nascent state. There was a strong push for Yiddish, since many Jews living in Israel at the time were European Ashkenazi. A few believed there should be no national language at all. More, of the Ben Yehuda vein, lobbied for Hebrew, which was said to be the true voice of the Jewish people. Today it is the official language of Israel, alongside Arabic.

As the conversation turned to the evening's exploits, I remained steeped in thought. Gazing out the window past brightly lit hotels, catching glimpses of the hidden sea, it occurred to me that baseball mirrored both Hebrew and Israel in interesting and as yet unrevealed ways. For example, both baseball and Hebrew had been resurrected in this holy land, though it took the game several thousand years longer.[1] Contemporary Israeli Hebrew was quite different from its ancient counterpart, but this change was arguably necessary for its rebirth. Similarly, baseball in Israel was different from its original form. Here we played seven innings instead of nine, tie games were settled with a home run derby, and fields only approximated the real thing. Maybe this change was necessary if the game was to flourish in Israel as had modern Hebrew. Perhaps we were the Ben Yehudas of baseball, I ruminated.

How about Israel itself—how did the IBL mirror Israel as a nation? It seemed that both had superimposed a pragmatic reality on top of somewhat conflicted origins. Despite those who denied Israel's right to exist—who actively fought against it—and apart from normative arguments on either side, the state had remained through myriad wars and conflicts. It had found a way to persevere. In similar fashion, in spite of many early difficulties the IBL had endured. There were one and a half fields to begin the season with six teams attempting to play six games a week. The vast majority of Israelis had never heard of the game of baseball. There was nearly a strike. A player almost died. Our television

1. It is thought that a ball game, perhaps similar to baseball, was played by the Israelites.

contract with Arutz Five Sports had been canceled. There was a dearth of bats and balls. The league nearly ran out of money—no, the league *did* run out of money.

There were also problematic theoretical parallels in origin. Israel's involved the notion of a democratic-religious state. What happened if the non-Jewish population, which was approximately 20 percent, should in the future become the majority? Was the identity of the state wrapped in a national religion? If so, was Israel more of a theocracy than a democracy? Was it possible to have a secular state while holding on to a Jewish essence? As Rothem would add, the only other Middle Eastern state that conceived of itself as a religious democracy was Iran. Likewise, if the league was only 30 percent Jewish, was it a Jewish league at all? Did the IBL want to be the best *league* possible or the best possible *Jewish* league? If it was the former, the percentage of Jews would drop precipitously, and few would not be Dominican. There might be ten Jews total. On the flip side, if the latter was paramount, then the talent of a Jewish-only league would decrease to somewhere around the level of junior-college baseball (which is not bad, just not professional).

Thus far, it seemed, the implications of these questions had been manifested in the bifurcated makeup of the league itself. There was an extremely large gap in ability between the most and least-talented players. We had triple-A guys competing against others who probably wouldn't make a good high school team. Perhaps, like choosing between a secular democracy and a religious nation, neither option was attractive. So Baras and the gang, like Ben-Gurion and the founders of Israel, opted for some combination of the two: a pretty good league with a fair number of Jews, the athletic equivalent of a Jewish democracy. For better or worse, then, on top of the theoretically shaky foundations of both the IBL and the state of Israel, a pragmatic reality had been built. I was standing on both, grateful, happy as heck to be part of the ride.

This all occurred to me, strangely, driving to the bar. Most of it anyway. The seed had been planted and would continue to germinate for the remainder of the season.[2]

When the cab finally stopped in western Tel Aviv in front of a large, dilapidated structure bustling with young people, I snapped back to life. Hopping out of the front seat I handed forty shekels to the cabbie. The last time I was here had been two years ago on Birthright. Our group stayed across the street at the regal Dan Panorama, but we never went to the Clara because of a *pigua* that had killed forty people several years earlier. Walking along the sidewalk, I once again saw the tall triangular Jerusalem stone memorial inscribed with the names of the victims. During Birthright we were too scared to go to the club. This time I hardly thought twice, but noticed that exposed wires and metal beams still protruded from the tattered roof, a vestigial reminder of the underlying danger of the land.

Trading an air-conditioned cab for the humid desert night, Levy, Wigg, Mike, and I followed a crowd left around the outside of the building. There was a huge mob smashing against the outside gates of the Clara. People squeezed against the railing, shouting, flailing their arms in the air, waiting to get called in. Petite girls wriggled to the front between strange legs; guys jockeyed for position. It was like a herd of cattle pressing against a feedlot, like the pit of the stock market with people screaming offers, some of which are occasionally accepted. For some reason the notion of orderly lines had been lost on Israelis.

Fortunately, early in the summer we discovered the trick: speak English. Israelis like to think of themselves as citizens of a fifty-first state. They are as pro-American as citizens of any other country to which I've been. Thus, we would jostle as close to the front as possible and say something, anything, in English. Being the

2. If this discussion is at all thought-provoking, check out Tom Segev's book *Elvis in Jerusalem: Post-Zionism and the Americanization of Israel*, trans. Haim Watzman (New York: Metropolitan Books, 2002).

tallest, I would raise my arms, tilt my head, and calmly shout, "We're here," as I did this time. Though brazen, the approach was quite effective.

A cute blonde manager standing on the railing pointed in my direction. "YOU."

"Fellas," I called behind me, giving a head nod plus a little smile to the guys.

Two large bouncers approached the gate and opened it just enough so we could slip through the crowd. What a mess. There have been few times in my life when I've felt like a rock star, maybe none. But going out as an American in Tel Aviv, much less an American athlete, was a unique experience. Several weeks later I would encounter a girl using the same trick to get into another bar.

"Hey, where you from?"

"Israel," she said with disdain.

"Then why are you speaking English?"

"Because zey always let zee Americans in. It is no fair." Evidently, our English-speaking gambit was not much of a secret.

Proud and confident, we walked into a scene much belied by the building's facade. A beautiful wooden deck hung over the Mediterranean, whose emerald water was illuminated by bright spotlights. The Clara was an open-air bar with white tables, sofas, the occasional canopy, and several swings. It gave one the impression of an enchanting Middle Eastern sanctuary, save for the reproachable techno blaring from giant speakers. The only thing more attractive than the place itself was its denizens. Many Israeli women were wearing a combination of white pants and tank tops, contrasting seductively with their bronze skin. No one seemed to be worried about another terrorist attack, though it was mildly disconcerting knowing forty people had been the victims of a suicide bomber here several years before.

We approached the bar and ordered four Goldstars, the most popular beer in Israel (the local domestic, Maccabee, being too unpleasant for even the most ardent patriots). Down below, around a cluster of booths, we encountered some players. One of the smoother Dominicans was lounging on a sofa, a girl in his lap. His trucker cap was pulled down over his eyes, and he was attempting to suppress a large grin. Some of the younger guys were dancing on a table, peacocking, swinging their silver chains, yelling how awesome this place was. I said what's up to the fellas and took a lap.

Walking around, it appeared that the Clara had been rebuilt off to the side of the original building. While a decrepit structure remained in front, this beautiful bar, more like a lounge, was constructed in back, fusing the old and new in somewhat disjointed fashion. Sure, there was probably some deeper meaning to all this, but reflection time had ceased. I just wanted to get a heat on, relax with the boys. And with the help of a few more Goldstars, this is exactly what I did.

28 The Road to Peace

Palestinian officials said Saturday that President Mahmoud Abbas and the prime minister of Israel, Ehud Olmert, would meet Monday in the West Bank city of Jericho. It would be the first meeting of the two leaders in Palestinian territory.

New York Times, August 5, 2007

THE DAY AFTER A START ALWAYS CALLED FOR A LONG run. But I happened to despise running. It wasn't so much the physical exertion as the lack of mental stimulation. On long runs I'd go crazy, thinking about nothing, anything, everything. Yet it came with the job. If you wanted to pitch, you had to learn to run distance.

Back in the day I tried radios, then Walkmen, then CD players, all of which worked okay. Then along came the iPod, a runner's dream. Stick it in your shorts or on your arm, throw it on shuffle, and blast off. Mos Def, Sam Cooke, Amos Lee, each song a new adventure. I found music one of the best ways to stimulate the mind while working the body. But perhaps best of all was good old-fashioned conversation. Tried and true, Luddite friendly, running with an interesting partner could not be beat.

Thanks to the cyclical life of starting pitchers, Rothem had thrown the day before me, and we were both looking to get in a good sweat. Fortunately, in the midninety-degree desert heat, this would be easy. We arrived at Kibbutz Gezer several hours before our game with Modi'in. On the bus ride Rothem and I talked about going for a run, so as soon as we disembarked, after schlepping our gear to the dugout, we took off.

Out the left-field gate we ran past the familiar swath of sunflowers, my old friends, onto a chalky gravel road. We climbed a small hill, winding past a ramshackle olive oil manufacturing plant. Many kibbutzim still produced wonderful agricultural products, but it appeared as though Gezer was now mostly residential. Nonetheless, the grounds remained speckled with trees.

As we ran, Dan and I talked about the league, Bruce Springsteen (his favorite artist), and his experience as the first-ever Israeli to play Division I baseball in America. But given our surroundings and his current job at the Center for Middle East Peace and Economic Cooperation, I wanted to talk with him about the conflict.[1] In addition to baseball, this occupied a majority of my thoughts during the season. Though I taught high school social studies and was completing a master's degree in political science, if anyone could speak articulately about the cleft between Israelis and Palestinians, it was Rothem.

Past the residential complex the gravel road became asphalt, and its pitch flattened.

"So, Dan," I began, "suppose you were teaching my students. In simple terms, how would you frame the conflict?"

He paused for a moment, as if to collect his thoughts. "There are four main issues when considering final-status negotiations: borders, Jerusalem, security, and refugees."

"What do you mean, 'final status'?"

"I mean, in the end, if there is ever a solution, it must involve these four facets."

---

1. For a more detailed, cogent, accurate depiction, skip the rest of this chapter and read Dennis Ross's *The Missing Peace: The Inside Story of the Fight for Middle East Peace* (New York: Farrar, Straus, and Giroux, 2004).

"What about Israeli settlements? Isn't that an important issue?"

"Yes, but it is usually folded into the border discussion."

"So borders as in post-1948, 1967, etcetera?"

"Yes, the Green Line was established by the UN in 1949 after the War of Independence."

"Which Arabs call *Al Nakba*."

"Yes, the Catastrophe. Point being, this is a key issue in negotiations. Wherever the border lines are drawn is extremely important to both sides."

Interestingly, Rothem was working on creating what would become one of the most detailed Israeli-Palestinian border-map databases in the world, about which he would deliver presentations to Israeli and American officials and think tanks alike. In short, Dan knew his stuff.

We passed a guard shack, and the labyrinthine road began to straighten, pointing us down a long, undulating strip of blacktop toward the main highway. It was HOT. Sweat dripped from our brows, and I wrapped a shirt around my head to prohibit the ubiquitous liquid salt from stinging my eyes. But I was not hating the run; my mind was occupied.

Dan and I continued to discuss the additional three components of the conflict. We talked about how in the 1947 Partition Plan for Palestine, the United Nations envisioned Jerusalem as an internationally administered city, a *corpus separatum*, about how prior to 1967 East Jerusalem was still in Jordanian control, about how the city had belonged to both peoples, multiple peoples, for hundreds if not thousands of years.

Concerning security, Dan mentioned that Palestinian statehood must happen in such a way as to not put Israel at greater risk. After all, Israel's historical narrative claimed that ever since independence it had been consistently attacked by hostile Arab nations, hence its use of force in the Occupied Territories and beyond.

In a similar vein, Dan noted that if Palestinians were to agree to a two-state solution, they must be satisfied with a just resolution to the issue of refugees. This, he said, was the linchpin, what stopped most negotiations dead in their tracks. Since there were an estimated eight hundred thousand refugees as a result of the 1948 war, a number that had grown through progeny into the millions, both reparations and repatriation were all but untenable from an Israeli perspective. Yet Palestinians demanded something of this sort in a comprehensive plan for peace. Even if borders, Jerusalem, and Israeli security could be successfully negotiated, both sides reaching an agreement on the issue of Palestinian refugees seemed difficult to fathom. But then again so did playing baseball in the middle of the desert, in the middle of this geopolitical conflict, in the Middle East.

Dan and I reached the highway about twenty minutes into our talk, stopping for a quick stretch. We turned around, saw waves of heat rising from the rolling asphalt, and chuckled.

"Why did we run so far?" I asked.

"Because you ask too many fucking questions," Dan retorted with a smile.

"No, it's because you're so long-winded," I shot back. "No wonder nobody can agree on anything over here. Everyone is too bored from listening to the other speak."

"What do you suggest? It's complicated."

"How 'bout a best-of-seven series? Winner gets Jerusalem."

"Okay, then, what about borders, security, and refugees?"

"There's always next season, Dan."

As for Rothem's sincere solution? Land for peace. He said it worked with the Egyptians and Jordanians and could work with the Palestinians, probably the Syrians as well. It would look something like this: Israeli agreement to a Palestinian state in most of the previously occupied territory (with some minor annexation of large settlements located near the Green Line, in exchange for an equal amount of land swapped from Israel proper to Palestine),

Palestinian recognition of Israel, and the subsequent signing of a mutual nonaggression pact or peace treaty or both. Sounded simple, but if so, there would be no need for ongoing negotiations, let alone Dan's cartographic legerdemain.

When we returned, Modi'in was taking infield-outfield. We got dressed, went through our pregame throwing routine, and settled into the dugout to watch our Lightning defeat the Miracle 3–2. At least somebody could beat them, I thought sarcastically after the game. Little did I know I would face Modi'in yet again in my very next start. Yikes.

29 Home Run Derby

WE HAD HAD TWO DOUBLEHEADERS ALREADY THIS season. The first was against Modi'in, the second versus Netanya. This would be our third, with the fourth coming the very next day. INSANE. To recapitulate, we had eight pitchers, while most professional teams playing a similar number of games carried twelve. Why we had doubleheaders at all, with six teams playing six games a week, was a mystery. Well, maybe it wasn't. Sportek, on which we were playing, was not completed until weeks into the season, forcing the league to postpone numerous games. In addition, there were several ties called on account of both darkness and encroaching upon Shabbat. In any case, we had some games to make up, which did not bode well for an already overburdened pitching staff.

To make matters worse, we were playing Modi'in yet again. Though our head-to-head record this season was fairly close (even with my own dismal performance), they swept us during our first doubleheader, setting an unfortunate precedent. In the first game of this double dip, Matt Bennett beat us 5–0. And I had all game to try *not* to think about the fact that I was 0-2 versus the Miracle, that back-to-back losses would exacerbate our chances of finishing first or second in the standings. Those were septic thoughts on Start Day. It was about staying relaxed, focused, confident, dry. Even under the blue-tarped dugouts in the midday heat.

On the bright side the Dominicans Eladio Rodriguez and Adalberto Paulino were sidelined due to injuries. I suspected the afternoon doubleheader had somehow hastened the momentary impairment of otherwise rock-solid athletes, but there was no way to be sure. Regardless, it helped tip the scales, put one in our column. The baseball gods had given me a chance. Plus, a rosin bag materialized at Sportek: another portentous omen. No more complaining about sweaty fingers, no more excuses. This time it was up to me. Both events, thankfully, boosted my confidence.

Perhaps because of this I threw well. Regularly ahead in the count, my off-speed could have been more consistent, though I walked only one hitter. It was like that scene from *Bull Durham*. Nuke LaLoosh has been struggling mightily, so Crash Davis, the wily vet, instructs him to wear a garter while he pitches (the rose goes in *front*, big guy). With Nuke's mind on the garter, thinking it's the secret to all big leaguers' success, his body is free to perform as it knows how. Similarly, with my mind on the rosin bag instead of my last two outings, my body could go to work. After every couple of pitches I'd grab the chalky sac, tap it against my left hip, flip the bag up the back of my hand, letting it roll down my arm to sop up accumulated beads of sweat, then pop it up, catch it, flip it once more in the air, and toss it against the back of the mound.

In the end we won 5–1, though it was much closer until the bottom of the sixth when Fish, Jeff, and the guys gave me a bit more padding. After the game I didn't yell, or cuss, or chuck my mitt. I just walked up to Wigg coming out to greet me, shook his hand, then turned around and got in line to high-five the rest of the guys. I had done my job. The streak was snapped. The garter worked.

The very next day we completed our last doubleheader. Two weeks before, tied with Ra'anana 5–5 after seven innings, the game was called for darkness. (We were lucky Sportek was built in the first place, and lights were clearly too much to ask for.) So before commencing our regularly scheduled game, we had to make up the tie, which was to be settled with—what else?—a home run derby. The decision to end contests with a derby had been decided early on by league officials attempting to make the game more exciting. This was also one of the reasons games were seven innings instead of nine. The league figured Israelis were more accustomed to the frenetic pace of soccer and basketball, so they wanted to make baseball more appealing. It was rumored they were also flirting with starting each count at 1-1 in order to further speed up the game. Thank goodness that was never approved.

Upon arrival we warmed up, took a quick BP, and then got started. There would be three hitters per team, six swings per hitter. Since Sportek had an abnormally short porch in right, about 260 feet at its base, the strategy was to pack your team with lefties in hopes they would have an easier time going yard. Thus, it was no surprise Ra'anana selected three lefties. For us Skip chose two lefties, Hastings and me, plus Brito, the All-Star Game home run–derby champ.

Ra'anana was up first, and their leadoff managed two home runs. Not bad. For us, muscle-bound Jeff hit first. He strolled to the plate wearing a scowl and his black Oakley sunglasses. A good strategy, I thought. Jeff had several home runs on the season and could very well provide us a big lead. But he didn't hit any. He scorched several line drives, just couldn't get anything in the air.

The second hitter for Ra'anana sent two more over the right-field fence. I was up next, down four to nothing. Walking to the plate I looked out toward Skip standing behind an L-screen about halfway between home and the mound.

"Just get the bat head out and drive it."

I nodded. Skip picked up several baseballs from a nearby bucket and got ready to throw. On the first pitch I took a huge hack, popping out to shallow right. One down. The second pitch I crushed. We turned to look; Lightning shouted from the dugout: "Get outta here!"

It left the yard, but several feet foul. Two down. The third and fourth pitches I hit weakly on the ground, trying to do too much. I'd become overzealous, opened my hips and shoulders prematurely, and rolled over two BP fastballs down the heart of the plate. This was one of the great paradoxes of the game: the harder you swung, the less distance the baseball traveled. Many hitters will tell you some of their farthest home runs come after they've barely swung, that at the glorious moment of contact it all seems so easy, effortless. Then you say to yourself, "Wow, you hit that a mile and you barely even swung. Imagine if you really put some force into it!" So you swing harder, only to hit two weak ground balls while your team is down 4–0 in a home run derby that will decide the fate of seven innings prior. I won't mention the next two swings. We were still down four to zilch.

Ra'anana's final hitter knocked out one more, which meant Brito had some serious heavy lifting: five yaks in six swings. And not for nothing: we had eight games remaining in the season, vying to win, place, or show. A preposterous derby or not, the final score still very much mattered.

Brito strolled to the plate, sans hat, like the All-Star Game. He dug in, taking the first pitch for timing. The second he took yard, gone no question. Brito took another. The next pitch was blasted to left, traveling toward the foul pole.

"Go, ball, go! Leave!"

"Stay fair!"

It did and we cheered. 5–2. With four swings remaining it appeared we might have a chance. As had become his rhythm, Brito took another pitch. He fouled the next one off, bad swing. Stepping out of the box he took a deep breath, his ursine figure emitting raw power and courage. He'd have to go three for his next three. If anyone could do it, it was Brito.

"Come on, Pupoooooooooo!"

"*Yalla*, Breeeet!"

"Let's go, Stuey!"

We were laying it on, trying to support him.

Skip grabbed a pearl from the bucket and nodded, grooving one down Main Street. Brito cocked his hands and hips, took a big step, and unloaded. The ball launched from his bat, screaming on a flatly arched path somewhere between a line drive and a pop fly. It climbed into the air, ascending until reaching mid–left field, then started to fall. Brito's uppercut—an attempt to lift the ball over the fence—had generated topspin, causing the baseball to decline more rapidly than normal. It landed about thirty feet from the wall. And just like that, the derby was over.

We impugned the process immediately.

"Stupid idea."

"This really is the Israel *Bush* League."

"How do we lose a game on a home run derby?"

"Ridiculous."

Ra'anana was rightly loving it. You won by the sword and died by the sword. It wasn't the derby's fault, or the league's. It was our own. Nonetheless, maligning both helped take the edge off, released a little steam. We still had a *real* baseball game to play.

Adding insult to injury, we were facing Esequier Pie, Ra'anana's ace All-Star Game starter, former Minor Leaguer for the Marlins, and one of the league's best arms. He stood six foot three with big hands, long legs, and a pugnacious demeanor, the prototype pitcher. He'd already thrown two no-hitters in fewer than ten starts, an absurd accomplishment. Last time Pie faced us, a Nate Fish infield single was our only hit. When he was on, Pie was deadly. In his arsenal was a low-nineties fastball, a slider, and a mystery pitch, the Vulcan, a permutated forkball/change-up. He held the Vulcan between his middle and ring fingers, Spock-like, making a circle with his thumb and pointer finger. Thrown with great arm speed, it exploded from his hand like a fastball, the bizarre grip causing it to slow and sink at the last minute, compelling hitters to swing foolishly over the top.

The secret to beating Pie, however, was patience. He had a penchant for wildness, walking hitters, taking himself out of the game mentally. If you could draw a few walks, move runners over with a bunt or ground ball to the right side, maybe punch one to the outfield for a sac fly, you had a chance. It was all about manufacturing runs against this dominating pitcher. And it was all about being *patient*, which we were not.

We knew his pattern, that he tried to get ahead with a fast-ball and then work the off-speed. If we sat back, making him throw two consecutive strikes, odds were he'd fall behind and be unable to throw the Vulcan. Sounded easy, but it wasn't. We simply could not hold back, could not abstain from pulling the trigger. No matter the location of that first pitch, in the dirt, in the eyes, off the plate, we'd swing. Once he got ahead with the fastball, we were toast. Perhaps an overly aggressive mentality had been set during the derby. Who knows? Either way he made us look silly.

Through three innings Pie had a no-hitter. We looked awful. In the fourth, however, Pie walked the bases loaded. Three guys in a row. Then he struck out Fish. Up next was Brito, who swung at two fastballs out of the zone. Skip was livid. He gave us the plan, but we couldn't execute. The old sage had been around this game so long he could virtually predict the outcome of particular situations. And he wasn't happy with Brito's approach.

Standing in the third base coaching box, he walked to the

on-deck circle, where I was getting loose. "He's going to strike out right here," he said matter-of-factly. Skip shook his head and went back to the box, not bothering to see Brito swing through strike three.

Walking to the plate, this was a shot at redemption. I felt terrible letting down our team during the home run derby, and especially since I already had one grand slam on the season, this could make up for my dismal performance. First time up I K'd without so much as taking the bat off my shoulder. Trying to be patient, I took several good pitches. As I approached the batter's box in the fourth inning, this was my chance to clear the bases, break the tie, give us a lead. Instead, with the bags juiced and Pie on the ropes in a crucial moment, I struck out to end the inning, leaving us nothing to show for a golden opportunity.

From then on, Pie was unhittable, literally. He tossed his third no-no for our second loss of the day. This doubleheader thing was not going well for the Lightning. With seven games left, approaching season's end, Modi'in nipped at our heels while Bet Shemesh was pulling out of reach. That light at the end of the tunnel, as the Israelis say? It may very well have been the train coming the other way.

30 *Tikkun Olam*

I WOKE UP THE NEXT MORNING TO MY ROOMMATE playing video games on his laptop.

"Oh—good morning, Aaron." The room was dark, the shades drawn.

"Hey, Joey," I said softly, in a fog. Rubbing my eyes, I slid on board shorts and a pair of gray rubber slippers, heading directly for the water closet, literally the size of a closet. Relieved, I walked outside in the morning sun. As my eyes adjusted to the bright light, squinting, I partook in a luxurious feline stretch. By the looks of the quiet halls, it was early.

Returning to the dim room I sat on my bed, searching for some clarity.

"Guess what, Aaron?"

I took a slow breath, preparing for conversation. "What's that, Joey?"

"They have all the stats online!"

"I know."

"Last time I pitched they gave me four earned runs instead of three! That's wrong; I need to go talk to somebody!"

"Yeah."

"I haven't thrown many innings, and this is really messing up my ERA!"

I laid down, unable to start the engine, and looked at my phone: eleven o'clock. Not early at all, except perhaps for ballplayers.

"Hey! They also have the league-leader stats here! Wanna know where *you* are?"

I leaned on my side, facing him. "NO."

"You sure?" he said with a smile.

I sat back up. "Yeah, no thanks, Joey. Process over product."

"Huh?"

"Never mind. Thanks, though. Think I'll just wait till the end of the season and see how I did then."

"Oh . . . okay."

"Hey, what video game is that?" I tried to change the subject.

"*Grand Theft Auto 4*. Wanna play?"

"No, thanks. I'm gonna get some breakfast." I threw on a shirt and headed up the road to the caf, past a mother peacock and her muster of chicks, stopping first to roust Hastings.

Inside, the mess hall buzzed lightly with clanging silverware and the familiar low hum of conversation. We sat down next to Levy and the rabbi-in-training, fellow left-handed pitcher Jason Bonder.

"'Bout time," Levy said.

"What are you talking about?"

"Camp, man."

I paused, the cerebral cobwebs evidently unshaken.

"Baseball camp? You know, the thing they're making all the players do?"

"Oh, fuck, please no."

"Ahhhhh ha!" Hastings started laughing. "You guys have to do that today?"

"What do you mean, *you* guys? If I'm in, you're in."

"No way. I've done two of those already," Hastings said. "Have fun—be sure to bring plenty of water, and sunscreen."

As part of the league's mission to spread joy to the people of Israel through baseball, players regularly conducted camps at Sportek. This was an integral part of the Jewish notion of *tikkun olam*, to heal and repair the world. Often, *tikkun olam* was revealed through community service. On Birthright, for example, we spent a day painting an elementary school in Rosh Ha'ayin (though I exhausted a majority of our time hooping with the kids). In truth, *tikkun* was an ethic about which I felt strongly. He to whom much is given, much is expected, as they say. The game of baseball had given me much more than I'd ever given back, and taking part in a one-day camp was the least I could do. Nevertheless, complaints of our woe were part of the fun.

Though there was a national infrastructure, the Israel Association of Baseball (IAB), of which Rothem would later become a board member, had tentacles few and shallow reaching. There were simply not many people in Israel, outside the nascent IBL, who knew much about the game. As it turned out, Levy, Bonder, and I would learn this lesson abjectly from a man named Mordecai.

When the three of us arrived at Sportek, a gaggle of kids was playing catch down the right-field line. In foul territory was an older African American gentleman who, upon seeing us, sauntered over to the infield grass. He wore shorts, a faded white T-shirt, and a dusty Yankees cap hanging like a yarmulke from the back of his head, revealing a scalp of thinning hair. "Hey, man. What's up, baby! Mordecai. Nice to meet you."

We exchanged greetings and introductions. Mordecai told us he made *aliyah*, or immigrated to Israel, from Minnesota several years earlier, taking a Hebrew name upon arrival. A delightful potpourri of culture, his colloquial African American vernacular juxtaposed in charming fashion with his Hebrew heritage.

Passion for baseball secreted from Mordecai's pores, and though he was the IAB's representative at the camp, after a few minutes it was evident he knew little about the game. He informed us there would be three stations, to which Bonder, who had worked camps previously, objected immediately. Bonder believed there should be one group composed solely of Israelis who didn't speak English, while two other bilingual groups rotated among several stations.

"Cool, baby," Mordecai said. "Whatever you like."

Bonder, who was proficient in Hebrew, took his group to right, while Levy and I headed with Mordecai and the rest of the pack to center field. Among others we had Dude, a religious kid with a yarmulke and tzitzit; Fifty-four, wearing a generic T by that number; Mussina, who wore a Yankees jersey; Sammy, a girl, hands down the best athlete; Rex Sox, who wore a Red Sox hat; and Yotam, the Tel Aviv Lightning batboy.

"Okay, we got two stations," Mordecai began. "The first is diving! These kids is afraid of the ball. We gotta get them to learn to dive! Second station is ground balls. But I want these kids getting down on one knee! Too many balls is going through their legs!" Mordecai dropped to a knee, tucking his glove just under his crotch like a catcher blocking a curve in the dirt: the antithesis of proper form.

I flashed a frightened stare at Levy, who grinned in embarrassment. The Arch Conservative was known to laugh inappropriately in situations deserving of greater tact, such as this. But Levy let loose only a muffled chuckle as we decided on the best course of action. While Mordecai was breaking kids into groups, I approached the team mom preparing snacks and asked who was in charge. It was unclear if Levy, Bonder, and I were running the camp or simply assisting. The team mom indicated she didn't know, that she was just there to ensure everyone was taken care of and well fed (like a good Jewish mother). Thus, Levy and I were faced with a Thoreau-like moment: if the baseball instruction was wrong, were we obliged to disobey it? After a short chat we decided in the affirmative. Levy took his group to the infield to teach grounders the right way—he was, after all, an infielder—and I stuck with Mordecai for damage control on the diving station.

"Keep your eye on the ball, baby! You gotta squeeze that glove! Squeeze it!" Mordecai was repeating this refrain while kids ran several steps and jumped toward a ball thrown just out of reach. After more than a few minutes of running, diving, smiling, rolling over, falling down, laughing, scraping knees, and banging elbows, everyone took a water break. Mordecai's heart was truly in the right place; he simply lacked the necessary acumen. When our group returned I directed several additional outfield drills. The kids stood several feet away, sprinted in my direction, and attempted to catch a ball dropped at their feet: the shoestring drill. Then they lined up for wide-receiver pass patterns, looking over their shoulder at the last minute to hunt down a ball in midflight: the tracking drill.

For the remainder of the morning, while Mordecai, Bonder, and Levy continued defensive training, I took the pitchers to the bullpen for a mini clinic. We broke down the six steps of a windup, practiced our delivery in unison, and competed to throw the most strikes. Afterward we partook in a well-intentioned lunch by the team mom.

In the afternoon Mordecai split the kids into teams and began a scrimmage, at which point we surmised our *tikkun olam* was complete. It probably wasn't—wasn't even close—but we had to return to the *kfar* in order to prepare for another game with the Blue Sox. The three of us thanked the kids, the team mom, and Mordecai, then hopped in a taxi. On the ride home it occurred to me that if baseball in Israel was to thrive, camps such as this were vital. But my experience illustrated that with poor teachers came deficient learning, that baseball would not grow without the necessary gardeners. Pick your metaphor—point being, baseball would be successful only with sound infrastructure, and sound infrastructure was possible only with knowledgeable individuals. From the looks of things, this would take some time.

It also occurred to me that I'd been too hard on Mordecai. He was a great guy, very kind and passionate; he cared about the kids and treasured the game. But he wasn't a baseball guy, and "Keep your eye on the ball, baby!" only went so far. The kids, for their part, loved every minute. They found in the game joy and delight, and perhaps this was all that mattered; perhaps this was our true mission. But informed instruction would only increase their enjoyment, let them experience baseball's wonderfully nuanced intimacies with which experienced players were so familiar. On that diamond the spirit was alive and well, but in order for the game to flourish, the execution of *tikkun olam* would need some work.

31 The Rookie

Israel is constructing a road through the West Bank, east of
Jerusalem. . . . The point of the road, according to those who
planned it under former Prime Minister Ariel Sharon, is to permit
Israel to build more settlements around East Jerusalem, cutting
the city off from the West Bank, but allowing Palestinians to
travel unimpeded north and south through Israeli-held land.

New York Times, August 10, 2007

EARLY IN THE SEASON SEVERAL OF MY TEAMMATES
began calling me the Rookie. After a game one evening we were
eating schnitzel and hummus in the caf when Josh Matlow, an
able, sturdy, hirsute Canadian outfielder known simply as Mat-
lock, learned I was a teacher.

"What? Ha, Pribble, you're the Rookie, man! Just like the
movie. A high school teacher, still shoving it."

"Yeah, right. That dude threw ninety-four miles an hour; I
throw eighty-four. Fat chance."

This was real life, after all, not the movies. Though the Hol-
lywood film was based on a true story, it wasn't my story. Thus
far the closest I had come to continuing my baseball career was
an offer from Wigg to play with him in Australia. He mentioned
it several times, said the coach for Ra'anana was his manager
Down Under, and since this guy was also a high school teacher,
he could find me work as a substitute. Wiggy said they played
only twice a week, and the rest of the time we could go to the

beach and carouse around Sydney. Plus, I'd live with him; we'd be boys, and the pitcher-catcher combo, the battery, would remain intact. Though I'd played baseball in Australia in high school, experiencing several "firsts" there along the way, I never took the proposition seriously. It wasn't a step forward; I would rather just visit him sometime for fun.

To be honest, that I'd actually leave a fledgling career in the classroom to pursue a boyhood dream all over again had never entered my thoughts. This was summer break, an adventurous escape, and I had every intention of returning to school. That is, until I opened an e-mail near the end of the season from the league president, Martin Berger:

> *If we are able to get you into the Atlantic league for the month of September, are you interested? I know you have to go back to school. Let me know.*
> *Martin Berger*

The Atlantic League, seriously? This was the best independent baseball league in the country, considered by many the equivalent of double A.[1] Ricky Henderson played there. So did Jose Canseco, Ruben Sierra, Juan Gonzales, and on and on and on, literally hundreds of players with Major League experience. Occasionally, big league teams even pulled guys straight from the Atlantic League into the Show. It was legit high-caliber professional baseball. Portions of my first two summers after college I had played in the independent Western and Central leagues, respectively, but the Atlantic League was king of the hill. This was an opportunity *not* to be taken lightly.

Sitting in the library at the *kfar*, where I wrote daily journals that would provide the basis for this book, I could only stare at

---

1. Independent leagues are professional—players are hired, fired, and receive a salary—but they are not affiliated with Major League clubs. They are also not part of any farm system, only tangentially linked to the ladder leading from single A to the Show.

the computer screen. Martin would need an answer, but how could I give him one? I typed several responses, wrote the words *yes* and *no* just to see how they looked, ultimately deleting each in kind, settling instead upon some noncommittal middle ground. Eventually, I replied:

> *At this point I cannot say for sure one way or the other, but it certainly is something I would be interested in considering. I understand this is a vague answer, but this is only because it is a difficult decision. If I can attempt to be clearer, please let me know.*
>
> *Thank you for the consideration,*
> *Aaron*

I didn't think I would sign but wanted to keep my options open. This was the pragmatic approach, the responsible one. But crazier things had happened. I'd made unexpected if not impetuous decisions before. I was three months away from attending law school, I remembered, had a tuition deposit and room assignment at uc-Hastings in San Francisco, yet decided while playing one last summer in France to become a teacher instead of a lawyer. That was a sharp left turn on the road of life, and maybe this would be too. I had exited the Freeway of Dreams for a brief detour—now was my chance to jump back on. String a couple of good seasons together in the Atlantic League, get picked up by a club, and from there anything would be possible. I was only twenty-seven, not much older than the average age of most rookie big league pitchers. And I could always go back to high school, or on to law school. But then again I'd worked extremely hard at my new craft over the past three years, dedicated this part of my life to teaching, much like I'd devoted earlier parts to the game. I had a new passion, but my old love refused to disappear. Conflicted, in a pickle, my mind raced back and forth between sides. Looking inward, the outcome remained uncertain.

As days passed and we marched through the season I was

pulled in alternate directions, the slightest memory, emotion, experience tipping the scale until another countervailing detail restored the problematic equilibrium. Though I could not have known it at the time, my decision would not come until setting foot on American soil one day after the end of the season.

32 Clinched

Cracking down on growing signs of dissent in Gaza, the Hamas
rulers on Monday broke up what Fatah-led opposition leaders
insisted was a peaceful rally for freedom of expression. The
Islamic militant group Hamas seized power in the Gaza Strip
two months ago, routing Fatah forces there.

New York Times, August 13, 2007

This was my final start. With four games left,
Skip wanted to throw me just a few innings to stay sharp since
I was slated to pitch the first game of the playoffs. Surprisingly,
this would be my first against the Netanya Tigers, having thrown
four times against the Blue Sox, three against the Miracle, and
once versus both the Express and the Pioneers. Netanya was in
the middle of the pack most of the year, sandwiched between
us, Bet Shemesh, and Modi'in on top and Ra'anana and Petach
Tikva on the bottom. As is the case in baseball, perhaps more
than any other sport, any team is capable of beating any other
on any given day. Netanya had several good starting pitchers, a
handful of sluggers, and Hector De Los Santos, besides Franco
the best defensive shortstop in the league.

With only several days' rest before playoffs, I wanted to keep
my pitch count low. Anything over one hundred pitches would
require more than a brief respite, so the number of innings would
depend on the number of pitches thrown. When I left in the third

inning it was 5–0, Lightning. No runs, no walks, two hits, seven K's. The only problem with strikeouts was the relative increase in pitch count (plus strikeouts were fascist, said Crash Davis, ground balls more democratic). Significantly fewer pitches were required of ground outs and pop flys. Plus, putting the ball in play kept infielders awake, involved, less likely to commit an error. Having thrown fifty-three pitches in three innings, buttressed by a five-run lead, I was pleased. Our team was in a position to win, and keeping down my pitch count set up nicely my first playoff start. Since we played seven innings instead of nine, pitchers in the IBL needed to throw four innings to get the win instead of five. That I'd come up one inning short crossed my mind, but I did not give it much thought.

In the fourth Crabb entered and got knocked around a bit. The score went 6–1 and then 7–2, and in the bottom of the fifth the Tigers battled all the way back to tie the score. As had happened more than a few times at Sportek, the game was called because of darkness: a 7–7 tie. This was a bummer since we would need to win two of our last three to secure second place. Only if there was a tie between us and Modi'in would we make up these last two innings with Netanya.

There was a buzz elsewhere around the league, however. Scotty Cantor, Pilates instructor and Petach's elder statesman, had just thrown a complete game to beat the Miracle 6–2. Thus, our magic number had become one, with three to play.

The following day we squeaked out a win against Bet Shemesh in the bottom of the seventh. With one out and runners on first and third, having pulled to within a run, they were threatening. A modest fly ball was hit to Jeff in right, and the runner on third tagged up. It looked like the Blue Sox would tie the score. But in a moment of Machiavellian genius, Frankie pretended to field a ground ball, suckering the runner from first to second, dekeing him into leaving early.

Playing first, as the ball sailed over my head I jumped a few steps off the bag, turning around to line up for the cutoff home. As the runner prematurely evacuated from first, I shot back to the bag and yelled toward right, "Jeff! Hey-hey-hey!"

Hastings caught the fly and was about to fire it home when he saw the play developing in front of him. He discontinued his crow hop, repositioned, and gunned to first as I stepped on the bag for the third out. But controversially, Bet Shemesh thought the runner on third reached home before I touched first, which meant the run would have counted and the game would be tied. We didn't think so, however, and neither did the umps. Sprinting to the infield for a momentary celebration before lining up to shake hands with our team, we had clinched second place. Since the Blue Sox clinched first one day prior and we were fairly certain Modi'in would finish in third, the playoffs were set, save for Ra'anana and Netanya battling for fourth.

That night after the game I was in bed, showered, brushed, reading a book. I was dosing, rereading the same line, my eyelids disobediently heavy.

Bang! Bang! Bang!

Startled by the loud knock I popped up and opened the door to find Fish, Levy, and Wigg waiting morosely outside.

"We need to find Jeff," Fish said. "Something's wrong."

I threw on some shorts, and we headed down the hall, asking around for our buddy.

"He's up the road."

Someone mentioned there was trouble with his family. My heart sank into my rising stomach, blending together a troubling stew of emotions. Jeff had given up a lot to play baseball in Israel this summer. He had a four-year-old son, Jayden, whom we lovingly referred to as Bamm-Bamm because of his purportedly super-human strength, much like his father. Hastings also confided in me that he was expecting a second child, another boy, several months after he returned home. It was hard to leave his young family, but, especially since his wife was cool with it, he couldn't pass up such a unique opportunity.

The four of us walked to his room, banged on his door. The lights were off, and we figured he might be asleep.

"Jeff?" we whispered. Nothing. "Jeff? Jeff. Hey, Jeff!" We called out louder but no response. I climbed up the wall onto a ledge behind his room, peering in. He wasn't there. We wandered around for a while, through the halls, on the outskirts of various rooms, then headed toward the caf.

In the middle of the road we found Jeff crying, collapsed on all fours. Our friend and Bet Shemesh's third baseman and manager, Eric Holtz, was there with him. Levy, Wigg, Fish, and I looked at each other, thinking the same thing, unable to speak a word. Earlier in the day Jeff had received a phone call saying Jayden was sick but that they didn't think it was anything serious. After the game Jeff was Skyping with his wife in the library when she said to hang up and call on the phone, away from everyone else.

Jeff was heaving. Between convulsive, shuddering breaths he stammered, "My . . . grandfather . . . passed away today. He had a heart attack . . . and died." It seemed to take all his strength to expel those few words. He tried to stand but was unable, settling into a catcher's squat. My first instinct was relief that Jayden and the baby were okay. But Jeff was in tremendous pain. We stood there, unsure of what to say or do, attempting to comfort him with our presence.

Eventually, we pulled him up and walked over to the benches between some trees on the side of the road. With a roll of toilet paper, Jeff grieved. He began to talk, which seemed to take his mind off the tragedy. His mom gave birth to him when she was seventeen, he said, and his grandpa Larry was like a second father. He had known him for thirty-seven years, longer than many know their own parents. Jeff harbored some remorse for playing this summer because he knew his grandpa was sick, and it was hard for him to be in mourning so far from home.

We sat with him for a long time, mostly listened, sometimes recounted a story of our own, doing our best to be his surrogate family in this distant land. I told of my grandpa Harry, whom, shortly before he died, I visited in Los Angeles on a drive home from independent ball in West Texas. I arrived late at night after hours of driving, and he came out to greet me. We embraced, and I walked inside for something to drink. Opening the spartan fridge I found two things: several Guinnesses and a tub of chocolate pudding. At first a bit concerned, it later made sense. He was living just the way he wanted—still smoking, drinking, eating junk food—and no one was going to tell him otherwise. Jeff's grandpa Larry, he said, stopped smoking more than thirty years earlier, but nevertheless a tumor developed in the bottom of his lungs, inhibiting his breathing all the same. We were both intimately aware of the long, slow death associated with years of smoking. Through the final days of the season, we all tried to be there in every way possible for Jeff.

Before our game the next day I approached Skip. "Hey, Skip. Jeff's grandpa passed away last night. He was pretty close to him. He still wants to play, in order to keep his mind occupied." Jeff had intimated as much to me the previous night. "But I still thought you should know."

"Thanks, Aaron. You bet." Then Skip changed the subject. "Well, I tried, but I think Feliciano is going to beat you for Pitcher of the Year. Your ERAs are about the same, and you both have seven wins. I was going to leave you in the whole game versus Netanya to get your eighth, but oh well. Maybe your 8-2 would have edged out his 7-1—who knows? But he was also on the team that won the league and had a few more strikeouts as well."

"Thanks." I kind of shrugged it off.

"I think there will be a chance for you," he added. "They'll take care of you after we're done here."

"Not bad for a washed-up high school history teacher, huh?"

He chuckled. "No, more like *The Rookie*."

We both laughed, and then got ready to play.

33 A Day in Palestine

LIKE A SONG, MY MIND WAS ALREADY IN PALESTINE. I had been thinking about this unfamiliar land the entire summer. With playoffs approaching it was now or never; we were running out of time. This was my chance to live it. Finally, at long last, Fish and I were headed to the West Bank.

Eating in the cafeteria before heading off, heads shook and good-byes were offered as if Fish and I would never be seen again. Crabb had been talking about going, but as our plans solidified, he backed out. "See ya, mate. Good luck. I hope we don't have to look for another pitcher and third baseman. On second thought, Pribble, do what you like. I want to be our number one. Fish, make sure you get back safe."

Scotty Cantor was eating with us too. He looked nervous. "Last week I was driving by the Wall of Separation with my cousin," he intoned. "I asked him what would happen if a Jew went to the West Bank . . . He said he'd be killed for sure. Do you guys really know what you're doing?"

Some bozo leaned over from another table. "You guys are fucking crazy. You're going into the nest of terrorists?"

We couldn't tell if he was joking. I hoped he was wrong. Either way, it was clear there were multiple perceptions of this foreign land.

Fish and I packed up our courage and a few belongings and took a *sherut* from the Central Bus Station in Tel Aviv to its counterpart in Jerusalem. The air-conditioned ride through the hills was short, pleasant. Upon our arrival the sun was close to setting, signaling the commencement of Shabbat and thus the closing of most stores, which would not have been a problem if Fish had not needed to heed nature's call. After scurrying between empty shops, Fish eventually found an open McDonald's with clean, spacious restrooms. He was back to normal five to seven minutes later, grinning like a spring chicken. Perhaps America's global empire was not so bad after all.

From there we took a cab to the Old City. We were dropped off just outside Damascus Gate, the entrance to the Muslim Quarter, and entered in search of lodging as the sky grew dark. We settled on the New Hashimi Hotel and Hostel, which I remembered from Birthright a few years before. New Hashimi rose above the melee of the crowded streets, culminating in a peaceful open rooftop veranda, overlooking the Dome of the Rock and the cramped housing below. Fish and I ascended immediately. As we climbed steps to the terrace, a heavy bass beat grew louder and louder, complemented by an enchanting flute rhythm. Beneath us an Arabic wedding party was under way. An immense courtyard enclosed scores of men crowded tightly together. Some were sitting, many were dancing, arms over each other's shoulders, and one was being hoisted around on a chair. It was a joyous environment, unlike anything I had ever seen. Though I was unaware of it at the time, this mysterious fete, and our night in the Muslim Quarter of Jerusalem more generally, served as a cultural acclimatization for what was to come.

The next morning we awoke to a small breakfast. In some ways the feeling in my gut was like preparing for a start. There was a healthy dose of anticipation, with some nerves and a growing focus. I thought about the rest of the guys back in Tel Aviv, still sleeping off a rowdy Friday night. That was not for us, not this time. Fish and I were headed out, following my friend Susan's instructions. Susan was a gal from Birthright I had discovered was living in Ramallah, working for a nongovernmental organization. I remembered her as short with close-cut dirty-blonde hair. Several days before she e-mailed directions:

> With your back to Damascus Gate, walk straight so that the Four Seasons restaurant is on your left. That is Nablus Road. Go one block up and you will see a bus station. Get on the number 18. You will pass through Kalandia checkpoint. You will probably not have to show your passport, since you are coming into the West Bank. If you do, the soldiers might try to scare you and say it's unsafe. Just be confident and say you are visiting a friend. When you pass through Kalandia, give me a call so I know when to meet you. Take the bus all the way to the end of the line and I will see you there.

As directed, Fish and I headed up Nablus Road, getting turned around only twice before running into the small depot. I had imagined a decrepit, beat-up bus with people smashed together, dirty windows pried open, no AC, and farmers on the roof holding chickens and cucumbers. In reality, however, it was fine. We found our bus, with a white "18" written between Arabic writing on a green sign. We paid 5.20 shekels, as there is no separate Palestinian currency, and jumped in. Fish and I sat next to each other in a two-person row. We even had our own fans blowing cool air.

On the ride we barely spoke, exchanging a few passing comments in low voices, occasionally looking at each other with fleeting grins before turning away. Whether this was due to nerves, excitement, or fear, I'm not sure, but I never once thought about turning around, like during the frenzied car ride to the Dead Sea. We were on the bus and on our way.

Just when I thought we could not be stopped, we were. The Kalandia checkpoint, exactly as Susan described it, was an ominous gray fortress — a big, gross pile of cement. At the entrance was a tall observation tower with dark octagonal slanted windows facing toward the ground. The line entering Israel proper stretched nearly a half mile in the opposite direction. Fortunately, the line entering Palestine was significantly shorter, though it moved at a snail's pace. We Slinkied toward the checkpoint: gas-break-gas-break-gas. Very slowly, bumper to bumper, we continued past the checkpoint. Our bus was not searched, and no one seemed to care about identification. Once through Kalandia, we met a one-lane roundabout in which cars converged from different directions.

I looked at Fish. "Dude, we're in the West Bank."

"*Dude*."

On the Palestinian side of the wall we noticed several stenciled images from Fish's favorite public artist, Banksy. One featured the black silhouette of a girl holding four balloons in an outstretched arm, floating toward the sky. Another was a colorful tropical-paradise montage that appeared to materialize from the cement, prying it open. A final stencil featured the portrait of a girl in a head scarf. In red just to the right of her face, in block letters, it read, "I AM NOT A TERRORIST."

The ride to Ramallah was slow and arduous, but it passed in an instant. I was captivated by the continuous construction, occasional street vendors, and a group of kids throwing rocks at a lamppost. I wondered why they weren't in school; it was probably summer vacation.

Arriving at the bus station everyone piled out, so Fish and I did the same. I called Susan, but she had overslept. I had woken her up. She instructed us to walk toward the city center, saying she would be there shortly. Fish and I approached a buzzing hub of five or six roads extending outward from a minaret. At the axis was a large alabaster statue of two proud lions. Above, like spokes on a bike, Palestinian flags splayed out in each direction. There were people everywhere, including security personnel in various uniforms brandishing AK-47s, and Alladin-esque caricatures pouring black coffee from oversize brass spouts. At first blush, Ramallah looked much more like a city than a war zone. There were clothing outlets and ice cream shops, hardware stores, office buildings, and apartments. More than anything, I was struck by the normalcy of the place. In this unfamiliar land, lives appeared more similar than different.

Eventually, Susan rolled up wearing a Canadian tuxedo (denim jeans and jacket), and we exchanged handshakes as instructed. "Sorry we can't hug," she said. "It would be inappropriate for a guy and a girl to do that here in public."

In a sweet twist of irony, our first meal in the West Bank occurred at an American café called Sinatra's, in a quaint Christian section of the city. For some reason I ordered lox and a bagel, which I had not once eaten in Israel. Sinatra's seemed a bit out of place, but we learned the owner was a Christian Palestinian who at one point lived in the United States. Susan also casually mentioned that she had been kidnapped six months prior. Excuse me?

Susan was a relatively fearless person, having traveled extensively in Zimbabwe when Mugabe was fucking shit up, so it didn't surprise me to learn she was living in Ramallah. Nonetheless, after being there for less than an hour, I was a bit taken aback by her account. Susan recalled the winter evening in a taxi outside Jenin, one of the more dangerous West Bank towns, as she played tour guide for two other friends. Oh, great, I thought. She said cabbies often picked up their buddies while giving customers a ride, so when it happened that night, Susan did not think twice. But when the taxi turned around and headed in the opposite direction, they got worried and asked the driver to pull over. When the taxi didn't stop, her two friends started screaming. One had the bright idea to jump from the moving car. Though Susan didn't agree, she figured since she got them into it, she should be a good friend and jump out along with them. As soon as her friend opened the door, the passenger in the front seat pulled a gun, saying "STAY THERE" in terse English. He then handed Susan a cell phone. The guy on the other end waited until Susan spoke first, to which he replied, "My friend needs something. When he gets what he wants, you will be free."

They were taken to a house, served tea, and taught Arabic to pass the time while their kidnapper began negotiations. Susan later learned that the man was a resistance fighter who was injured by the Israeli army. He was not able to receive medical treatment and evidently thought abducting Americans was his last option. The three girls were finally released when the Palestinian Authority agreed to pay the abductor's medical bills and give the man a job *as a policeman*.

Strangely, I felt safer after hearing Susan's story. Never mind that the only person I knew here was kidnapped, showing around two friends much less. When I learned that the girls were used as a bartering chip, as a sort of currency in a broken economic system, that they were not seized in anti-American hatred, I was reassured. I did not condone the deed, but I could understand it. Would I commit a heinous act to support my family or in order to survive? I hoped I would never have to make that decision.

After our meal we left the Christian neighborhood and climbed a road circling the spokes of the city. It was a nice walk, and we could see small towns in the hilly distance. I envisioned Ramallah as being hot and sticky, but it was actually quite pleasant, with a regular floating breeze, much like Jerusalem. We crested a moderate rise and encountered the Muqata, the Palestinian White House. This was the spot where Yāsir 'Arafāt had been put on virtual house arrest by the Israeli Defense Force during the Second Intifada. Susan said the compound was converted from an old British-mandate prison. As the hill began to level we passed an opening on our left with a booth and several guards. We kept walking. A block farther we turned the corner and came upon yet another opening. Two young guards stood in front of us with large guns and ferocious expressions. Susan spoke to them calmly in broken Arabic. Her words apparently did the trick, and we walked in.

"What's up, guys? Thanks."

As Fish and I passed the guards their expressions flipped, their faces lit up, and they began speaking to us, in turn, in broken English. "Hey, man, where are you from?"

"The U.S. — California."

". . . and New York."

They nodded, impressed. "Okay, thank you, welcome," they said, ushering us forward.

In the compound we reached yet another set of heavily armed guards with the same result. Susan said we wanted to enter, and the guard replied, "You want to see the leader?" It struck me as an interesting turn of phrase, but we said yes and walked in. On the far side of the courtyard was a large memorial. Another guard followed, and we stood there for a while, looking up at a huge poster of 'Arafāt's face and a marble book covered with a yellow flower wreath below. Staring toward the cenotaph I heard the guard's words in my head: "The leader." It occurred to me that the line between terrorist and freedom fighter was fuzzy. Perhaps both labels were simultaneously correct: a mutually inclusive contradiction, a manifestation of the dueling Palestinian and Israeli narratives. For my part I attempted to refrain from judgment, trying simply to understand what reality was like for Palestinians in general and these soldiers in particular, though it was not easy.

We left the compound. We were almost across the street when the two young guards stopped us. "Hey, come." It gave me a start, and I immediately looked at their big black automatic rifles. But they just wanted to know why we were there.

"Paying our respects," said Susan.

"For education," I replied.

"Yeah, we think it's interesting," added Fish.

They seemed to be pleased with our answers, appreciative of our interest in their lives. "Okay, bye. Have fun," they said as we walked away.

Returning along one of the spokes into downtown Ramallah, Susan told a story about the sexualization of eye contact in the Muslim world. She had run into trouble one day with her neighbor and unfortunately learned her lesson the hard way. During a conversation with the man and his family one afternoon, she looked him in the eyes, thinking this was the polite thing to do. He interpreted this as something other than respect, however, and showed up outside her apartment late that same evening, expecting a secret tryst. From them on, it was more than awkward between the two neighbors. After hearing this story I felt a heightened sensitivity to the people around me. I tried not to look anyone in the face, but it felt unnatural. As women walked past, nearly categorically covered in head scarves, I noticed an intentionally subtle yet distinct aversion of the eyes.

I began to think about how people were looking at *us*, even if women did not make direct eye contact. Fish and I made somewhat of an odd couple wherever we went anyway. His flowing, leonine, Samson-like mane and prominent facial features combined with my height and short arms tended to attract attention. Folks would check us out, occasionally swiveling their heads as far as humanly possible, but I perceived these looks to be of interest rather than malice. From the security guards to the nut wholesaler to the peddler of *knafa* — a traditional Palestinian dessert — people seemed genuinely happy with our being there; in fact, the smile was the expression of the day. Fish and I both commented that we felt very safe, though also a bit out of place (I will not say like "fish" out of water).

After a professional eating tour of the city we were all fairly pooped, so we returned to Susan's place before our evening excursion to Bethlehem. Following a quick rest, we were off. Just outside her apartment on the way to the car, in the late-afternoon sun, we noticed a couple of kids playing in the street. They reminded me of the little Israelis at our games, pestering us for balls incessantly. But these two just shot us a glance and looked away. Grabbing a baseball from the bottom of my bag, I called one of them over.

I kneeled down. "Do you know baseball? Do you like it?" I said, flipping the ball in my left hand. The boy didn't speak English. I handed him the ball, but he wasn't quite sure what to do. So I performed a throwing motion in the air and told him to try. "*Yalla,*" I said. He flipped it to me. Nice! I motioned for him to back up toward the middle of the street. He did, and we began tossing the ball back and forth. Within two or three throws he became proficient, grinning with each bare-handed catch. All the while his little buddy was watching intently from the side. I waved him over, and he took my spot. Though a bit younger, he too figured it out right away. They began playing baseball in the street. From a window above, four more kids poked out their heads, hands clenched on the iron guardrail. They looked curiously at the exhibition below. A couple more and we got a team, I thought.

Eventually, it was time for us to move on, so we all exchanged high fives. Fish, Susan, and I began to walk away, but the kid wasn't sure what to do with the baseball. "It's yours, dude. Keep it." I pointed to him and the ball. He grew very excited and flashed a small grin, his eyes surging with emotion. His little friend ran over and tried to grab the ball, fussing over whose it would be, like any two kids faced with the prospects of splitting a new toy. Fish and I gestured that it was theirs to share and walked away. After several paces, just before dusk in a small Ramallah alley, I stopped and turned around. They were throwing the ball back and forth in the street, having a catch. Goose bumps shot down my arms, tingling the back of my neck. We had merely given one baseball to a couple kids, and maybe it was only symbolic, but the seed of baseball was planted in Palestine. Perhaps someday children would throw baseballs instead of rocks. We could hope.

The night before in the Muslim Quarter we saw a CNN spot in which an Iraqi garbageman, holding up a deflated soccer ball and referring to his national team's recent victory in the Asian Cup, said, "This game has done more for my country than any politician ever did." Sports could unite people, bring them together. Instead of arguing about UN 181 or 242, I thought, maybe we should create an Israeli-Palestinian Little League. The path to peace might be ninety feet and four left turns. A couple liners, sac flies, and double plays, and who knows . . .

From Ramallah we drove through the Kalandia refugee camp, back along the wall, and through the countryside. Next to Palestinian villages stood Israeli settlements with Israeli-only roads. In my mind it was clear these settlers were actively infringing upon Palestinian land, that they were a key source of the conflict. Road 1 that we took to the Dead Sea several weeks earlier, for example, cut across the West Bank and was protected by the IDF. We had been completely safe, though we didn't know it at the time.

On the drive to Bethlehem, Fish and I received a call from our friend and Bet Shemesh manager Eric Holtz, who was checking to make sure we were all right. He joked that if we were in trouble they would call in reinforcements for Fish right away, but that they'd probably leave me until the end of the season. The Blue Sox couldn't risk another loss, he said.

We continued on, driving through the hills of Jesus's birth, until reaching Bethlehem. The three of us entered a community center where some of Susan's friends were giving a global refugee talk. It was an international crowd sprinkled with a handful of Palestinians. From across the street we bought some food and before long found ourselves watching an important yet hopelessly dull and entirely too long PowerPoint presentation. I hoped I wasn't like this in the classroom. Taking out my cell phone, I texted Rothem, who was in Jerusalem on business. I could not focus on the lecture, choosing instead to stare out the window toward a small Palestinian village, daydreaming.

When the presenters finally wrapped up, the sun had set and I was finished with my apple and plum. We went downstairs to mingle with, as Fish described them, a bunch of activists ready to start the revolution. They were very nice, genuine. We shared a couple Taybeh beers, the local Ramallah brew. Since we had a game the next day Fish and I decided to leave, even though everyone was headed to a party. With Dan set to pick us up on the other side, it should have been the end of our adventures. But in this part of the world, nothing was that simple.

After exchanging warm good-byes with Susan, we took a taxi to Gilo, the nearest checkpoint. I thought briefly of Susan's recent abduction, but was calmed when our cabbie began playing bland Top 40 pop on the radio. I asked him if he liked the music.

"Yeah, man. You?"

I told him yes because I didn't have the heart to say otherwise and he was excited to talk about America. We drove to the checkpoint with the wall on our left. The cabbie let us out fifty feet away, and we walked the rest.

"Peace out, man," the cabbie said.

"Okay, dude. See ya."

At the checkpoint three Israeli soldiers were illuminated by a flood lamp beaming down from the tower above. Though Gilo was smaller than Kalandia, from this side of the wall, in the dark, it seemed more menacing. As we approached, a car was being searched by one of the soldiers, and Fish and I advanced on foot. We received suspicious glares until saying what's up to the teenagers in camouflage. As much as the square blue documents we presented them, this refrain was our passport, signaling our American status. The soldiers pointed us down the road to the left, into the terminal. After walking several paces past the guard booth, Fish and I stopped to look at the Wall of Separation. Another car had just pulled up, and two of the soldiers were barking at the driver. We were in a purgatory of sorts, past the wall but still in the checkpoint. As we turned around, a giant rainbow-colored poster, floodlit by a giant spotlight, read "Peace Be with You" in English, Arabic, and Hebrew. I noted the irony.

Fish gave one of his characteristically deep, guttural laughs. "Haaaaaa, what the fuck!"

Reaching the terminal, we were the only two people present. It was deserted. We went through a tall metal turnstile and down a ramp. It felt like a cross between an airport and a cattle yard. I was glad we weren't there in the crowded morning heat, as was our original plan. Down the ramp we took a sharp left and entered a fortress. The room was a high-ceilinged, tall-walled, brightly lit maze (Rothem would say later that it was specifically designed so that if someone blew themselves up inside, the explosion would go up rather than expand, causing less danger to the soldiers placed carefully out of direct view). There were many doors, so we picked the farthest on the right after turning another corner. It was locked, and there seemed to be no one in the building. I gave a knock but nothing — it was silent. Fish and I looked at each other, confused, thinking we had taken a wrong turn somewhere.

Suddenly, a booming female voice radiated from above. "BACK UP AND GO TO THE RIGHT," it said omnipotently. "THE DOOR IS BACK AND TO THE RIGHT."

Fish and I looked at each other for a moment in shock, then burst into laughter.

"Dude, what the — ?"

"This is bananas."

We retraced our steps and somehow found the correct door. We went through and to the left, took a right, and stumbled upon a metal detector and adjacent bag-screening device. Peering to the side, through thick glass, we saw a teenage girl with her feet up. She could have been my student. It was like *The Wizard of Oz*. The thundering voice turned out to be a young, annoyed soldier from behind the glass. I smiled, waving, and she unwillingly broke into a grin as well. Her expression seemed to say, "I don't want to smile at you idiots, but I can't help it." I put my bag on the machine, which by this time had started running. Then I went through the metal detector, setting off a loud bell and red light. I immediately stepped back and put my hands up, fearing a giant robotic arm would snatch me away.

"JUST GO THOUGH. WALK THROUGH."

After taking a right turn and then another left, we encountered a row of turnstiles. We walked ahead, but the cold metal bar against my thigh did not move, jerking my entire body forward. I looked at Fish, confused yet again.

"GO TO YOUR LEFT AND STRAIGHT OUT THE DOOR," said the voice. But this time we heard a faint chuckle at the end of the command.

To our surprise, the door was in fact the exit. Outside at last, we jumped into Rothem's idling gray Mazda and drove off.

"Thanks for taking me, man. That was awesome," Fish said.

It was awesome. It was also unique, exhilarating, eye-opening. Between recounting events to Dan, I reflected on the day. If I wasn't an American, I don't think I would have felt comfortable speaking flippantly to the IDF. If I were a day laborer from Bet Sahour, Nablus, or anywhere else in the West Bank, I certainly would not have been giggling as I passed through the Gilo checkpoint on my way to work. I would have felt like one of a million cattle herded from turn to turn, then dumped outside. As much as this made me feel angry, it also made me feel safe. If the borders were not protected in this way, it would be much easier for dangerous people to enter.

As calm and peaceful as it was in Palestine, this side was Israel and I felt at home. I felt safer but less secure, guilty about being happy, a troubled love. My conception of the Israeli soldiers was also problematic. On one hand, I had great respect for their work keeping the country safe. But on the other, I viewed them as the aggressor, often making Palestinians feel less than human and actively protecting the settlements that I was so fervently against. Yet another mutually inclusive paradox, it seemed.

Pulling into the *kfar* late that night I felt tired and satisfied. Traveling to the West Bank was the final thing I had wanted to do with my time in Israel. Well, almost the final thing. To quote the Indians' third baseman speaking to Wild Thing Vaughn in the movie *Major League*: "There's only one thing left to do . . . win the whole fucking thing." And with the playoffs upon us, that's what Fish, myself, and the rest of the Tel Aviv Lightning were trying to do.

34 Playoffs

Bottom of the seventh, two outs. I stroll to the plate with one runner on, down a run to Modi'in. Working the count full, I foul off two sharp Matt Bennett sliders. Then he tries to beat me inside, but I recognize it early, launching a missile to right center. As the right fielder races back, hitting the fence, the baseball sails feet over his head. There is pure elation at Sportek, the entire team awaiting my arrival as I approach home. I step exuberantly on the plate, everyone jumping up and down around me. We go nuts.

Or how about this: It's the top of the seventh, and I'm straddling the mound with two outs. Eladio Rodriguez, arguably the league's best hitter, digs in. It's one to nothing, the flamethrowing Maximo Nelson having given up only a solo blast to Hastings, leading off the game. From then on it has been twenty up and twenty down, a veritable perfect game. I wind up, and Eladio swings through a first-pitch change. Then he takes a fastball millimeters outside. After swinging through another fastball and taking another slider, the count is even, 2-2. I throw the slider again. This time it's a hair elevated, staying in the zone fractions of a second longer, and he swings over the top. Wigg catches strike three, charges the mound, and hoists me on his back as the rest of the Lightning, hands raised in euphoria, race toward us from the dugout and the field.

But neither event is true. They would be fairy tales, perfect endings. This was Israel, after all, and the reality was much more sobering, even strange. For our playoff game at Sportek it was oddly overcast, the sun struggling to break through intermittent clouds of gray. Whether the air was more or less moist I'm not sure, but the rosin bag, my garter, was parched, present, ready to dry.

Modi'in's leadoff popped to Sam at second to begin the game. With two quick strikes on him, the next hitter knocked a soft Texas Leaguer to right that bounced for a hit in front of Hastings. Jeff picked it up languorously, momentarily bobbling the baseball. Upon seeing this, the alert runner took off, snagging second before Jeff knew what had happened. Something small, an extra base here or there, was often all it took. Aaron Levin, the third hitter and first overall pick in the IBL draft, swung through a 1-1 slider that squirted past Wigg, allowing the wily runner on second to dash to third. The next pitch Levin grounded routinely to Frankie at short. He picked it up smoothly and flicked it across the diamond, short-hopping Brito at first. Pupo leaned down to scoop up the throw. But Sportek had other plans, errant and unpredictable. Instead of glancing the dirt, the ball leaped aggressively toward Pupo's face, smacking him squarely in the nose before rolling several feet to the side of the bag. His colossal body fell to the ground, legs twitching, inversely curled to the hazy sky. The runner, who had not been going on the routine grounder, took off upon Brito's malady. He scored easily.

Time!

Our substitute trainer, chatting aloofly behind the fence, made his way belatedly to first.

"Ice! Bring some ice!" our dugout yelled. The trainer stopped, started, stopped again, then directed someone else to the task as he jogged over to a writhing Pupo, face in the dirt. I meandered from the mound, not wanting to lose focus, but worried about my teammate's condition. It took several people to roll him over and, with stiff legs, sit him up. Blood poured from his ordinarily broad nose—now the shape of a *Z*—down his face and neck, onto his jersey.

After treatment they stood Brito up, red-tainted gauze on his face, and walked him off the field. It was a big blow to our team, let alone his mug. Levy, who was DHing, went to second, while Sammy moved over to first. With no designated hitter I was now batting as well.

Our new defense positioned, one out and one run in, Eladio walked to the plate. A characteristically aggressive hitter, he popped the first pitch down the right-field line, the shortest part of the field. Not again, not like Gezer, I thought. Jeff was playing even with second, deep in the right-center gap, a long run to get there. He raced over, building speed and approaching rapidly as the baseball descended, on a collision course with the obstinate fence. Sizing it up from the mound, it would be close. Mere feet from the sharp, vertically lined steel, Jeff stuck out his glove. In a frantic instant, he snagged the fly, crashing violently into the fence, bursting it open. The powerful force of impact, however, caused the baseball to bounce from his glove and fall to the grass, rolling back toward first. As Hastings swirled to pick it up his body jerked backward, as if on a leash. The fence had closed in on his jersey, trapping him, tethering his body feet from the foul pole. He yanked, tugged, stretched, wrenched, tried to move, tried to free himself from the ill-fated yolk, to no avail.

As the ump loped down the line, the runner on first sped around the bases, Eladio trailing behind him. Seeing Jeff's predicament, arm outstretched, unable to reach the ball, Levy cleverly ran all the way out to right, as the lead runner approached third. Levy grabbed the ball and fired it home, reaching Wigg moments after the runner crossed the plate. Following a heated discussion with both managers, after prying Jeff free from the fence, the umps ruled he did not have possession long enough to record the out, leaving two runners in with one out and Eladio standing on third.

The next hitter, Paulino, hit a sac fly to mid–center field, allowing Eladio to score easily. 3–0, I thought.

"He left early! He left early!" our dugout shouted.

Following proper protocol I toed the rubber for the next hitter. Stepping off, I threw to Fish at third in order to appeal Eladio's ostensibly premature departure.

"Out! Safe!" two umpires yelled in tandem, the third base ump pumping his fist as the home-plate ump spread his arms, palms down. Deferring logically to the one at third, I dropped the ball on the mound and walked toward the dugout, the rest of the Lightning sprinting in behind me.

After a meeting of the minds beyond second base, the umpires let the play stand, inning over. Right or wrong, the gods owed us a break after Brito's broken nose and Jeff's unintentional debacle in right. In perhaps the most bizarre inning of my career, we began the playoffs down two runs.

It would stay this way until the third, when the Miracle scored their third run, the second unearned of the game. We battled back with two in the fourth, but they picked up another that same inning on a solo home run.

And that was the final: 4–2. We were behind from start to finish. No fairy-tale ending, not like the movies, just a bit of the odd, the abnormal. A fitting capstone, perhaps, to a peculiar season. Just like that, it was over. For us at least. Modi'in would play the Blue Sox, who had recently beaten Netanya, in a one-game championship for the first-ever IBL crown.

After the game we walked down the left-field line for our final postgame chat. I straggled, late to leave my dugout chair, taking a knee on the outer circle next to Fish.

"Aaron—where's Aaron?" Skip queried, looking over and past us several times before finding me in the back, with the help of the team. "Good job today. Real good. You kept us in the game and gave us a chance. They should have got one, maybe two—that's it. What can you say? Nice job."

I appreciated his words. But they registered in vain against the anguished pit in my stomach, the patina of grief shrouding my thoughts. Skip went on to talk about the game, about how we needed to hit a little more in order to have a chance, but didn't dwell on the negative.

"You know, at my school, in our seasons, they almost always end in a loss. That's what happens, unless you win the championship. No one likes it, but it's part of the game." He proceeded to thank us all for being a part of his team, having a great season. He'd speak for a while, stop, then speak again, as if there were more he wanted to say, further emotions he wanted to impart, but he didn't, couldn't. "Okay," he said with a quasi-sentimental sigh, half looking forward, half already nostalgic, then brought us up and proceeded to shake each player's hand individually.

I sensed the emerging dispersal of our team. The bond of competition that held us so tightly together had changed, already partially disintegrated. The burgeoned relationships would endure, some more powerfully than others, but there would never again be another Tel Aviv Lightning. No more Brito and Levy and Fish, Langbord and Frankie and Hastings, this season more ephemeral than all others, though I could not know this at the time.

I wanted to express to Skip his influence, but, still tacking between disappointment and exhaustion, I froze, powerless. After shaking hands, everyone began to scatter. Still on a knee, lost in thought, I stood up. "Hey, Skip, hold on. Guys." We regrouped. "While we have everyone here I want to say something. Skip, there are a lot of managers in this league, but I speak for the team when I say you are the one true *coach*."

"Naw, there's others . . . ," he began humbly before Fish cut him off.

"No, he's right." Fish slapped Skip on the *tuchus* with his hat. "Our team thinks it, and the rest of the league knows, too. You're the real thing. We would not be anywhere near where we are as players, or a team, if it weren't for you."

Skip tried to brush it off, uncomfortable with public admiration.

"It's from us all when I say we want you to know just how much you've meant to us this season," I added.

His eyes became red, welled up. "Thank you." He walked over, stuck out his arms, and gave us a hug.

Afterward I went to the dilapidated dugout to change from my uniform. I grabbed a plastic green chair and headed into the twilight for a quiet spot to pack up my things, and my thoughts. I put away my glove, uniform, cleats, and towel, and stared out at the field, wondering if I'd ever take them out, ever again lace up the spikes or crack the mitt. I wondered how many times I had been in this spot, contemplating the prospects of my final game, not quite sure what to make of it, or how to feel. In college I cried my eyes out after our last match at Fresno State, sat all alone on the warm metal bench, hoping it would not be my last. In France I hit a homer my last at bat, celebrated joyously with a *gran fete* after the game. But here at Sportek I just stared into the outfield distance, void of emotional clarity, confused, unsure, until interrupted by a schnerfling Fish who, with tears in his eyes, pulled up a chair. We sat in silence.

Then he put his arm around my shoulder, gave me a squeeze, and slapped my thigh. "Good job, man."

"Thanks, dude," I said, exhaling.

We remained this way a while longer until hearing an Australian accent through the fence behind us. "Ay, mates. Tuborg or Carlsberg?" Wiggy was holding a tall red can in his left hand, a green in his right. He lobbed them to us over the fence. "Great season, Prib. Great job, Fish." Then he walked away.

"Wondering if this will be your last?" Fish asked.

"Yep. I've done this too many times. It doesn't get any easier." It was too soon to contemplate, the game still fresh in my thoughts. But I sensed instinctively the looming decision: quit my job on days' notice to follow a recently unearthed dream, or relegate this summer to mere memory, a flash in the pan.

About then some of the others walked up. We exchanged high fives, hugs, requiems. Hastings came over with his shirt off, gashes on his left and right shoulders from the crash. "Sorry, Pribs. I would have gone right through that fence for you. I had it. I had the ball, but the fence knocked it out."

"I know, man. I know you would have. At least now you got some nice marks to show for it."

We commiserated for a while, finished our drinks, then grabbed our stuff and headed to the bus.

35 All Good Things

In a belated move to erase the last vestiges of his short-lived partnership with the Islamic militant group Hamas, the Palestinian president, Mahmoud Abbas of Fatah fired dozens of Hamas-affiliated senior civil servants, an official in his office said Saturday. Those affected were hired last spring under a power-sharing agreement between the rival factions.

New York Times, August 18, 2007

AS OUR SEASON CAME TO AN END, SO TOO DID MY relationship with Yael. Several days earlier we made plans to get together after our game. She was to pick me up in her red Peugeot outside the *kfar* as usual. Walking up to meet her, past a particularly obstinate male peacock, I ran into Fish and Levy, who also wanted to go out.

"Oh yeah? Just come along," I said to them casually. "Yael's picking me up, so we got a ride into Tel Aviv."

"Nice, *yalla*."

Upon seeing the three of us pile into her car, Yael was less than pleased. I didn't think Fish and Levy could tell—they were jawing in the backseat—but her subtly pursed lips revealed a measure of disdain. Though our conversation was pleasant, I could tell this sabra had something to say.

It was only fitting, I supposed in hindsight, that we would return to the Port in northern Tel Aviv, the site where we had first reclined on outdoor sofas overlooking the Mediterranean, spittle from the sea landing intermittently at our feet. This time Levy, Fish, Yael, and I went to Shelvata, an outdoor beach bar with music and dancing, lined with sand, several establishments south of our initial location. A bit on the younger side and slightly cheesy, Shelvata was a fun spot nonetheless.

The night began well. The four of us chatted and people-watched, playfully judging others with an unironic sense of entitlement. Then Yael mentioned that Fish looked like Samson, the biblical figure who derived power from his hair, a parallel Levy and I had drawn at the beginning of summer. We loved it. "See? We told you!"

"Hey, how do you say *Samson* in Hebrew?" I asked Yael, trying to stretch the moment.

"Shimshon."

"Shim-shon?"

"Yes."

"Shim-shooooooooon!"

"Ah! What's up, Shimmy!" Just like that, Fish had a new moniker.

But as the night progressed Yael turned snarky, at first on the sly, then increasingly directly. Sighs mounted, my flirtatious grins repudiated with a callous averting of the eyes. I knew what was up, but did not want to discuss it at the bar.

When Fish and Levy became momentarily enmeshed in conversation, Yael leaned past my ear. "Why don't you just hang out with your friends?"

"Yeah, I am. It's fun."

"You should just talk with them."

"What?"

"*Aron*, you are clearly more interested in having fun with Nate and Jacob. I should go."

"No, come on. We're all having a good time. This is great."

"You said *we* were going to hang out tonight, not us and your teammates."

"I didn't think it was a big deal. Is it?"

"No. But I want to be with *you*. We don't get to hang out that much anyway, and now we're with your friends too." She paused. "*Aron*, tonight you either stay with your friends . . . or spend time with me. You need to choose."

I did not think twice. "Okay." I sighed, as if forced into a decision not of my own volition. "Let's walk you to your car."

"Walk *me* to my car?"

"Let's just walk to your car." We traveled north up the wooden boardwalk and crossed east over the river Yarkon near the power plant, arriving at a quiet parking lot, having uttered few words along the way.

I wasn't into having a "talk." This was the end of our season, the conclusion of the summer. With days remaining I wished to savor every moment. I had to follow my heart. I told Yael that with the summer drawing to a close our fate was uncertain anyway, and though I cared for her there was not enough time to split between her and my friends, let alone the game. If she wanted me to choose I would—in fact, it was clear I already had. She did not resist, simply turned over the engine and smiled reticently. I leaned through the window of her car and kissed her good-bye. In the moment it was unclear if either of us would call, if we would meet again during these last few days. I felt parts of us both secretly hoped so. But as I watched Yael pull away, wavy dark hair twisting over and around her seat, red taillights in the distance, it was the last of her I would see. No love at first sight, no heartache across continents, no fairy-tale ending. Somewhat like our season, it seemed.

Walking back to the Port I realized this was not the first time I'd made such a decision. In Hawaii I left Sarah, the only girl I had ever loved, to realize my goal of playing professional baseball on the mainland. Though we promised to stay together, our relationship did not last the summer. Back then my decision was obvious: I would follow my dream at whatever the cost.

Here in Israel, though of a different magnitude, my choice was equally certain.

On foot alone under the stars and feeling introspective, I remembered another song I had tried to write, this time about playing what I thought was my last-ever game in France. Inspired by Common's ode to hip-hop, it began:

> *She stayed with me when I was good, stuck by my side when I was bad*
> *She's given me so much*
> *I just wish I could give her something back*
> *She made my cry oh so many times, made my dreams come true*
> *She's all I ever wanted*
> *She gave me an education, showed me around the world*
> *She taught me so many lessons*
> *How many times I've played the fool, she kicked me out a time or two*
> *But in the end it's me who's quitting*
> *I just lost the love of my life*
> *As long as I remember, we've been together*
> *I just lost the love of my life.*

It was quite a shock to stop playing baseball. For more than twenty years the game was an integral part of my existence, then suddenly gone. I couldn't watch it, listen to it on the radio, or talk about it with my friends. Visceral images of playing in college, even high school, would visit my dreams without warning. Like the amputee who wakes up rubbing absent limbs, a part of me had vanished in France. Yet here I was playing again, scratching old scars, exposing fresh wounds, appendages magically resurrected, this summer one great tryst.

Approaching Shelvata, as timber creaked beneath my feet and the music grew louder, like choosing baseball over Sarah and Yael, I wondered if I would make a similar decision: revive my dream at the expensive of a practical, responsible career. To what ends of the earth would I follow my phoenix? At what cost? Perhaps there was a love story in Israel after all.

"Where'd you go?" Fish and Levy asked.

"I had to walk Yael back to her car."

"How come?"

"'Cause she said pick you guys or her."

"Seriously?"

"Yep. Here I am."

They smiled, and we slid deeper into the crowd.

And so all good things, as they say, must come to an end. So it was with Yael and our season. All that remained was the championship between Modi'in and the Blue Sox, as well as a minor decision about my future. Plus there were rumors of some informal awards ceremony that Fish had been talking about. But that would probably never happen. It couldn't.

36 The Schnitzel Awards

A BAR MITZVAH WAS A RELIGIOUS AND CULTURAL institution, a rite of passage. I'd never been initiated, unless one counted the guerrilla indoctrination in a Tel Aviv shul on Birthright several years prior. In the eyes of the ticket lady during the start of my trip, at least, this meant I was not Jewish, not part of the tribe, not yet a man. In fact, the opposite was true: this summer had brought me closer to my roots, nearer to my historical identity, much more a Jew. We could not let a similar travesty happen to this young league. Given its quasi-Jewish nature and disparity in talent and ability, the IBL desperately needed a sense of self. By the end of the night we would set a historical precedent, create an enduring tradition. To mix religious metaphors, the juvenile IBL would be christened into manhood. And there was no better way, it seemed, than to throw the league its own awards show.

To say "we" might be hyperbolic. An inchoate version of the idea was birthed back around the time of the purported desert rainout. Because of the league's general lack of organization and logistical competence, guys began organically referring to the IBL as the Israel *Bush* League. The fields were bush, the umps were bush, the payment system, living situation, and schedule were bush. And quite frankly, some of the players were bush too. We needed an outlet, a vehicle to expel our criticism both valid and illogical, to give our gripes their due.

Throughout the summer guys would quip, "That should win the award for worst call" or "I should get the award for best room," and so forth. Sometime toward the end of the season we were dining in the caf when it was mentioned that we should *actually* give out these awards, and the concept blossomed. But as far as I knew, this was just an idea, nothing more.

Thanks to Fish and the Nordau Street gang, several well-to-do players from the Lightning and Petach Tikva who decided to rent a flat in Tel Aviv rather than subject themselves to such substandard living conditions, the IBL would have its version of the Espys, Emmys, Tonys, and Oscars. Except ours would be called the Schnitzels, a tribute to the infamous staple cuisine at Chez Hawkfar. Since this would be a self-effacing awards show for the Israel *Bush* League, however, the winner of each category would be the bushest, not the best, and each would receive a breaded, fried, desiccated chicken patty on top of a paper plate, an appropriately dubious honor indeed.

Arriving at the *kfar*'s performing arts center adjacent to the library, Levy, Jeff, and I encountered a packed auditorium buzzing with excitement. The entire league was there, literally, along with Skip and his wife, several other coaches, Commissioner Kurtzer, and Martin Berger. The three of us descended stairs in search of a seat. Attendees were instructed to dress as bush as possible; it was especially important if you would be presenting an award, as I was. I hoped my white V-necked T-shirt, jeans, aviators, plaid green-and-orange Hawaii baseball visor, and kitschy tie would not disappoint. It was disgusting. Had the balance of the audience not been similarly attired, I would have been quite embarrassed.

On the raised stage stood Fish in a fuzzy-ball-topped green ski hat, hipster Nikes, and leopard-print Hammer pants, spinning funk records with his portable turntables and mini Marshall speakers set atop a baby grand piano. A slide-show montage was playing on the big screen behind him. Emcee for the night was Aaron Rosdal of the Nordau Street gang, laced in a "Don't Be a Fool, Stay in Hebrew School" T, a white suit, rainbow Adidas sneakers, red headband, black Prada sunglasses, and red nylon fanny pack. Rosie was a quintessential mensch, smooth, soft-spoken, and endlessly witty. I was Big A, he was Little A, and I loved him. Looking around the crowd, I noticed several guys in togas made of bedsheets. One guy was in a suit. Rees, that sexy Australian, wore only a Speedo. Crabb was sporting a dress shirt, tie, and board shorts. Somebody donned a Lucha Libre wrestling mask.

The room was insufferably hot, and I was already *schvitzing*. Though technically in breach of the Code of Conduct, players openly drank mufflers of beer. As Fish turned down his speakers, Rosie walked to center stage, quieting the audience for his opening monologue. Setting the tone for the rest of the evening, it was a hilarious performance no recounting could do justice.

To conclude he announced the categories. Up first was Call of the Year. The nominees: Petach Tikva forfeits because an outfielder is ejected and won't leave the batter's box; five Blue Sox are ejected simultaneously, including Eric Holtz, who yells at the umps, "I'm gone? I'm gone? No, *you're* gone!"; and, finally, ball four is called on Rey Rey while the pitcher plays catch with the short stop in order to stay loose. Ball four was proclaimed the winner, and the crowd cheered, though there was a collective moment of remorse for Reynaldo, who returned to the Dominican Republic several weeks earlier, because of his head injury unable to play the game ever again.

Next was Play of the Year. The nominees included: a Modi'in pitcher snuggling with his girlfriend on the bus, then throwing her batting practice between games of a doubleheader; Bet Shemesh's catcher yelling, "I'm gonna get you, bitch!" on an unassisted double play while the runner throws a batting glove in his face; the Modi'in player-coach inserting himself into the game to face Feliciano with the bases loaded, only to strike out on three pitches; and Wiggy taking a pop fly off his head, the ball nearly bouncing over the netting into the stands. The Blue Sox's catcher won, which, since these were the Bush Awards, was fitting.

Climbing the steps to the stage, I presented the Schnitzel for Coach of the Year. This went to the Pioneers' manager, one of the most successful Jewish pitchers in Major League history, who had already been sent home for poor behavior and disreputable comments to the media. For such an incredible Jewish athlete, he did not reflect well upon the league.

Adroitly juxtaposed, Skip, a true coach, would present the next award for IBL Employee of the Year. Among the nominees were Martin Berger, Commissioner Kurtzer, and a tattooed Burger's Bar employee smitten with a majority of the players. Before the winner was announced, however, a stranger appeared onstage dressed just like Skip during a game. He wore BluBlocker sunglasses, zinc oxide on his nose, a Miami Dade baseball cap, gray baseball pants, turf shoes, and a white towel tucked around the back of his neck into a blue warmup. The impression was spot-on. We could not keep it together, wondering who this interloper was.

"Ladies and gentlemen," Rosie declared, "Dane Wigg."

"Wiggy! Ha! Classic!"

The two Skips opened the ballot, reading it together: "And the winner is . . . Martin Berger!"

Martin came up to accept the award in good spirits. He knew there had been some bumps in the road, but he'd made a good effort to smooth them out along the way. Skip and Skip stepped aside for the acceptance speech.

"Thanks, guys. But seriously, I've got a lot to say." He collected his thoughts as if to deliver a heartfelt couplet on the trials and tribulations of this miraculous league.

But his pause was a second too long. Someone from the peanut gallery cracked, "Yeah, I'm working on it!" which was Berger's line for much of the summer. The audience exploded in laughter, and Martin, realizing his moment had passed, genially returned to his seat, Schnitzel in hand.

Next was Team of the Year. This went to Petach Tikva. It was not simply because they started and finished in last place; no other squad had such a collection of oddballs. To cite but a few examples: they set the record for most ejections, including their coach, who was expelled from the league, and players had been known to smoke outside the dugout during games. The entire bunch came onstage to accept their honor. "Hey, we finally won something!" a player shouted.

The awards continued. Ump of the Year went to an angry German known simply as zee Nazi. Over a Petach Tikva player calling the ump after his ejection a "fat fucking Jew," Kurtzer's instruction to simply "share the bats" after running out of lumber midway through the season, the Dominicans asking to "leave the night of the last game," and a Modi'in utility infielder telling his coach, "I can't play today—I have too many holes in my swing," Larry Baras, league founder and not in attendance, won the Schnitzel for Quote of the Year. He was overheard saying, "This has been the worst summer of my life."

Moving along, the Schnitzel for Biggest Blunder went to Sportek, which beat out the *kfar*, the idea of ending games with home run derbies, and the day that games were nearly canceled because umps, trainers, and television crews had not been paid. Uniform of the Year was a difficult category. A Ra'anana pitcher was nominated for throwing BP and coaching first in shorts and flip-flops, while a Ra'anana infielder, Brendan Rubenstein, was nominated for overaccessorizing, wearing multiple Livestrong bands, wristbands, tape, eye black, glasses, and two pairs of batting gloves all at once. From Netanya, Leon Feingold was nominated for pitching in one cleat and one *sneaker*. Bet Shemesh's owner was nominated for simply wearing a uniform, like fantasy camp. In the end the Schnitzel went to the aforementioned Modi'in utility infielder for wearing to batting practice a unitard consisting of a skin-tight Under Armour T-shirt tucked into extra-small mesh shorts pulled aggressively up his waist.

Finally, Player of the Year, the most (un)coveted award of the night. Among those in contention were the Modi'in utility infielder (again), Petach Tikva's outfielder, and the eccentric Neon Leon Feingold. The largest player in the league, thighs like tree trunks, his inability to locate pitches was perhaps more intimidating than his low-nineties velocity. Briefly a Cleveland Indian, and more recently a competitive eating champion, this was Leon's due. And he received it. As Leon walked onstage to accept the award, a big-screen video displayed one of his finer moments: punting his glove in the air toward shortstop after surrendering a home run at Sportek. Wearing a full suit for the occasion as if knowing he would win, Leon accepted the Schnitzel in stride. The crowd cheered him good-naturedly.

Since there were a handful of leftover awards, and all were well aware of Neon Leon's voracious appetite, we goaded him into eating the last of the chicken patties as fast as possible. "Le-on! Le-on! Le-on!"

He acquiesced. Taking off his coat and loosening his tie, Leon cracked open a tallboy of Tuborg and went to work, shooting his head back between bites as if mired in competition.

Once Leon was finished, Rosie drew the evening to a close, delivering some final remarks as Fish resumed spinning records. The crowd cheered mightily and then began filing out of the auditorium.

All said, the Schnitzels were a success, a better than expected opportunity to affably poke fun at the intimacies of a peculiar season, a once-in-a-lifetime summer. League officials struggled to make this dream a reality; players lived, ate, traveled with one another, competed day in, day out, except on Shabbat. A shared experience, a capstone, the night brought us closer together and gave everyone a chance to reflect on the beautiful maladies of the IBL. And the league itself had reached a cultural milestone, established, mature, bar mitzvahed, never again the same. The transformation was official; there were awards and tears of laughter as proof. We had no idea if the IBL would endure, but there was a tradition, a rite of passage. There were the Schnitzels.

37 Sportsmanship and Character

The inaugural Israel Baseball League season has come down to a championship game scheduled for today between the Bet Shemesh Blue Sox, managed by Ron Blomberg, and the Modi'in Miracle, managed by Art Shamsky. Blomberg's team finished first in the six-team league with a 29-12 record, then won one playoff game to reach the final. Shamsky's team finished third with a 22-19 record and had to win two playoff games.

New York Times, August 19, 2007

I WOKE UP TO THE SUN PEEKING THROUGH DRAWN curtains, just like any other morning. Except this was my penultimate day in Israel. The championship was tonight, followed by an official awards ceremony. I would be leaving the following afternoon, Monday, already late for school. That is, if I resolved to return to Tam. I had yet to call my principal, figured it best not to worry him. I'd cross that rapidly approaching bridge if necessary. As of this morning I had still not made a decision.

Grateful to forgo the standard caf fare, Hastings and I were going to be picked up by Rothem for breakfast. An Arab breakfast, hummus. Walking up the hall I encountered Jeff and Crabb sitting on the stoop at the end of the dorms, the latter with his laptop open as per usual. They both knew about my "process over product" thing, but our season was finished.

"So you want to know how you did?" Jeff asked. They both smirked.

"You know, I haven't looked at the numbers the whole year."

After our last game I'd forgotten, neglected to consult the league Web site for our final stats. I knew I'd thrown well, but then again, so had many others.

"You want to know?" Crabb asked once more.

"Yeah, you want to?" Jeff pestered.

"Um, sure, why not?"

"You-lead-the-league-in-ERA," they blurted, trying to be the first to divulge the surprise while attempting to mask their excitement.

"It was close," Crabb continued. "You just beat out Feliciano by a few tenths of a point, 1.94 to 1.97." Though shocked, it was nice to hear. I had no idea, hadn't even considered it. Still recovering from my final loss, our team's final loss, it made me feel slightly better.

"So, think you'll get Pitcher of the Year?" Jeff asked.

"I dunno." The possibility had not even occurred to me.

Ever the pundit, Crabb commenced his analysis: "You guys both led the league in wins, but he had one less loss. He also had more strikeouts, but you had fewer walks and pitched more innings. Plus, you threw against Bet Shemesh or Modi'in every time."

"Excerpt for two," I interrupted, feeling a little uncomfortable about playing the stats game.

"You should be Pitcher of the Year for sure," Jeff said.

Jeff would kill for his team; in fact, he literally ran through a fence for me. I appreciated his support. "I don't know, man. He was on the winning team and had more K's. Maybe it's a toss-up."

We continued guessing who would win various awards, interjecting interesting results.

"Can you believe Kramer hit .345?"

"How about El Ave? He led the league with *fifty* hits and had a .381 average. Frankie is legit."

Then Rothem texted from the front gate.

"All right, Crabbie. Later."

Like an episode of *No Reservations* with Anthony Bourdain, we set out in search of the good stuff, Jeff and I with our local tour guide, trekking off the beaten path for local cuisine at its unassuming finest. We drove south through Tel Aviv into Jaffo and entered a sleepy neighborhood, parking on a tranquil side street. Dan was taking us to Abu Hassan's, the best hummus joint around. Walking up a small incline and crossing over a shaded public courtyard, we came upon a modest establishment. There were no signs, just a takeout window and small eating space. Since we arrived too late for a table, the place already overflowing with people, Dan ordered our food to go. Several minutes later we received our bounty and followed Dan through crooked streets and alleys to a house in midrenovation overlooking the sea. Sitting on a low-lying rock wall, we removed hot Styrofoam cups, plastic bags of pita, and a package of raw onion chunks.

"You want to have it the *real* way?" Dan goaded us.

"Of course."

"I'm not sure you can handle it." He peeled a slice of onion, then scooped it through the stew of creamy garbanzo and tahini, into his mouth.

Jeff was alarmed, his upper lip slightly curled. "Can I just dip the bread in?"

"Sure."

I, on the other hand, was excited, diving in onion after onion.

"Don't forget about the sauce," Rothem added. He poured a tangy, slightly piquant liquid into his cup. Jeff and I did the same. The hummus was already far superior to any version I'd eaten in America, creamy and warm, with lumps of garbanzos and a tinge of fresh garlic. Adding the sauce, it became orgasmic, the flavors brought to life. They say a breakfast of hummus will last the entire day. Not only is it dense and stodgy, but mouthfuls of raw onion will fumigate one's palate hours into the evening. In my fervor to eat like the locals, I learned this lesson abjectly.

Bellies full, mouths blissfully tortured, and brows moist with sweat, we drove to Dan's workplace apartment, a beachfront penthouse-turned-office in Tel Aviv, in order to kill several hours before the championship game. This was a common hangout for Jeff and me over the summer, an escape from life at the *kfar*. Inside we reclined on leather sofas slightly sticky from the humid air. A leisurely breeze swept through open windows, and within minutes the three of us were asleep.

Sometime later Jeff and I awoke to the rapid typing of computer keys.

"What are you doing, Rothem?"

"Just a little work." I peeked over his shoulder and saw the border map about which he would deliver presentations in the coming months. How Dan kept a job during the season was a mystery. I could barely pitch once every five days. He was doing that *and* trying to solve the conflict.

Soon it was time to leave for the game. At the door Dan grabbed his Tel Aviv Lightning jersey and hat.

"What the hell do you have that for?"

"They told me to bring it. I think I'm winning an award."

"Yeeeaaaaaaah!" Jeff and I shouted, hugging Dan, standing uncomfortably. "Best Israeli—you know it!"

Dan demurred, said he wasn't sure, that maybe the pitcher from Netanya should receive it.

On the drive to Yarkon Field I received a call from Andrew Wilson, the slender league employee from New York whom I met on my first night in Israel. Along with Dave Rattner, who worked his ass off tending fields and resolving constant crises, Andrew was the veritable glue, the grease, the dude most responsible for keeping this league together. Assiduous and unremitting, it was the players' collective opinion that he should win an award for most valuable staff.

"What up, Andrew?"

"Pribble, be sure to bring your cap and jersey to the game. And could you tell Fish to do the same?"

"Yeah, you bet. Thanks. Bye."

"What'd he say?" Jeff asked excitedly.

"He said to bring my jersey and hat like Dan. Plus to tell Fish also."

I called Fish, who had already heard. "Dude, I think I'm gonna win the Sportsmanship Award. Great," he added sarcastically.

"Naw, you've got Best Defender locked up."

"I don't know, man. Hey—think you'll get Pitcher of the Year? That's what I've been hearing."

"I don't know." Discussion of awards was the gossip of the league, like high schoolers guessing who had a crush on whom, eagerly awaiting the revelation.

After a quick stop at the *kfar* we arrived at the championship game. There were several thousand people in attendance, the vibe much like Opening Day except for the lack of a television crew who had yet to be paid. It was exciting. Significant auxiliary seating had been added in the form of plastic green chairs, and most were already full. Without traditional stadium seating, crowds piled against the fence, leaning, straining to see the action. Barring some freak accident or biblical collection of plagues, the league had made it, finished the race. All in attendance were anxious to see how it would end.

The first pitch was thrown by some *macher* from the Jewish National Fund, one of the league's biggest sponsors. A second first pitch was flung by little eight-year-old Rudy Rubin, who, as the announcer noted, "had been injured by a terrorist attack. Thank God he is alive."

Both teams were announced. Feliciano, Rees, and Johnny Lopez received the biggest applause. Since Bet Shemesh and Modi'in had drawn the largest attendance this season, it was probably good for the league that both teams were competing for the championship.

The Blue Sox were throwing their number two: a tall righty with surfer-blond hair and broad shoulders named Rafi Bergstrom, the pitcher who plucked Wigg in retaliation for Langbord's home run, nearly causing a brawl weeks earlier. Intimidating Maximo Nelson was chucking for the Miracle. A sound match-up.

Maximo gave up one run in the first on a Jason Rees sac fly. The game would remain close for the duration. As goose eggs posted on the scoreboard, Jeff, Fish, and I meandered impatiently, feeling a mix of emotions, mostly remorse at not being out there ourselves. We began in the right-field bleachers, then moved behind the plate and everywhere in between. Fish was getting mobbed by fans, an iconic figure of the IBL. I noticed Levy had made his way onto the field, taking pictures like a journalist, as if he belonged. Later in the game, "Moish Lewis, from Jerusalem," was announced, just like Opening Day. Only this time it did not sound weird, novel, or out of place. I did not even find it funny. After the next inning they played that song, "War, huh—what is it good for? Absolutely nothing," and I thought of little Rudy Rubin, of the destitute children of Palestine, of Likud and Labor, Hamas and Fatah.

Seeing Skip, the three of us exchanged heartfelt handshakes with our manager. I did not know at the moment this would be my last time speaking with him. Skip handed us slips of paper with his handwritten contact info, photocopied, cut into the size and shape of regular business cards. It was poignant.

Steve Hertz
Head Coach Miami Dade College
telephone number, e-mail
address

"Isn't this the darnedest thing you've ever seen in your life?" he said, clearly nostalgic. "I would not trade this for the world, I tell you." Looking out over the field, the day's final light lying gently on the outfield grass, the smell of (kosher) burgers and dogs, it didn't seem like baseball in Israel, just baseball. Fans applauded big plays, made up cheers in unison—"Max-i-mo! Max-i-mo!"—and waited in rhythmic anticipation for crucial moments, important counts. Skip was right—this really was something. The game was healthy; it worked here.

"Aaron Pribble, to the scorers' table, please." Puzzled, I found my way over. The husky announcer cupped his mic, whispered, "You're the answer to one of tonight's trivia questions. We need you to sign a ball." He handed me a pearl and Sharpie.

"Sweet spot?"

"You bet." Most often the thin, rectangular area between the seams closest together is reserved for coaches, superstars, or those with a grandiose sense of achievement. It is more humble to sign beneath the horseshoe, especially if multiple people will be adding their names. Slightly embarrassed, I chicken-scratched the sweet spot.

During the subsequent half inning the PA declared, "And now for our next trivia question. Who led the league in ERA and tied for the league lead in wins?"

Crickets.

"Still looking for an answer. Okay, here's a hint," he continued. "He plays for the Tel Aviv Lightning. That's correct!" A teenager in Tevas, wire-rimmed glasses, and *kippa* jogged to the scorers' table to receive his prize. I pondered what this might augur for the upcoming awards ceremony.

The game neared completion. Bet Shemesh picked up two more runs indiscriminately, while Modi'in had yet to score. Since the championship game was nine innings instead of seven, Feliciano took over for the final two. With the last pop-up to first, a complete game shutout, the Blue Sox streamed from their dugout to celebrate with a much deserved dog pile near the mound. They were the best team, deserved to win. I was happy for them, but it stung. As the Blue Sox donned their crisp, newly pressed white "IBL Champions" T-shirts, I stole a glance at Fish and Hastings. Their expressions revealed a similar sentiment of regret. We'd dreamed of this moment numerous times, and it was difficult not to place ourselves in their shoes, to live vicariously, if remorse-fully, through their triumph.

Players from other teams breached the field, congratulating Bet Shemesh and Modi'in. Fans smashed against the fence. As the awards ceremony began the rest of the league receded to foul territory between the backstop and home. Modi'in was given the second-place trophy to hearty applause. When Bet Shemesh accepted their crown the stadium erupted: "Blue Sox! Blue Sox!" Fans screamed the names of their favorite players. Some threw wristbands and batting gloves into the stands.

Then it was time for individual awards. All grew quiet in anticipation.

"Up first, the home run king. None other than Bet Shemesh's own . . . Jason Rees!" He had homered in nearly half of all games, a remarkable accomplishment. Jason accepted his award humbly, and the crowd burst into Blue Sox cheers yet again. Rees picked up Best Defensive Outfielder as well, splitting it with Josh Doane of Netanya. Next up was Best Defensive Infielder. I looked at Fish kneeling by my side. He grinned.

"Best Defensive Infielder goes to Hector De Los Santos and Nate Fish!" I stood, gave Fish a sideways hug, and rubbed his head as he advanced to receive his award. Fish was touched. His passion for the game was uncompromised, and this honor meant a lot to him, though he tried his best to conceal it.

Best Defensive Catcher went to Eladio Rodriguez of Modi'in. Turning around midstride after receiving his award, Eladio returned to the middle of the infield to receive the batting title as well. He had edged out Greg Raymundo of Bet Shemesh. Both held remarkable averages, silly numbers for a baseball league.

It came as no great shock when Rothem was named Best Israeli. He hugged and high-fived Schlomo, the Netanya pitcher and only other Israeli to play Division I baseball in the States. Characteristic of Dan, he received the award begrudgingly. I'm sure he felt that "Best Israeli" was a slight, that he wanted to be the Best *Pitcher*, period. But deep down Dan understood the significance of the award for the league. It illustrated that Israelis could compete at a high level, even if they were few and far between.

"And now the Commissioner's Award." Just a few more, I considered, trying not to think about it. Why else would I have been told to bring my jersey and hat? I took from my back pocket a small pin with an Israeli and Palestinian flag joined at the staff, one of two I bought at the bazaar overlooking the Old City during our trip to Jerusalem. Taking off my Lightning cap, I tacked the pin underneath the thunderbolt, slightly off-center. In earlier visions I would pull an Israeli-Palestinian flag from my back pocket after winning the championship, waving it around the stadium in a symbolic gesture of peace, my own version of the Black Power salute at the 1968 Olympics. Like Tommie Smith and John Carlos I would use the sporting arena to advocate on behalf of a cause in which I believed deeply. "Be the change you wish to see in the world," I heard Gandhi say to me. It would be heroic. My defiance, my courageous deed, would make global headlines. The *New York Times*, CNN, even Fox News would beckon for comments.

But with no championship, no center stage, I settled for a pin on my cap. Winning Pitcher of the Year would make players, fans, and league officials notice my statement. At least they would know how I felt.

"This award goes to Brendan Rubenstein . . . and Aaron Pribble." I wasn't paying attention, caught by surprise, unable to move.

"Dude, they said your name," Fish whispered. "Get your ass up there."

Along with the überaccessorized Rubenstein, I staggered forward to collect my plaque, trying not to think of it as the Little League equivalent to the Coach's Award, the trophy for the kid you want to recognize even though he hasn't won anything. The teacher's pet. Make sure you smile, I thought. Pull yourself together. It's not embarrassing; act like you're grateful. After taking a picture with the commissioner I returned in a haze to my seat. Kneeling once again next to Fish, I wondered if anyone had noticed the political statement. I heard no chants of "Two states! Two states!" My heroism, valor, swept under the carpet of history. There would be no headlines, just an overlooked pin and a faux-gold plaque for sportsmanship and character.

The final awards passed in a contemplative miasma. Most Valuable Player was split between Eladio Rodriguez and Greg Raymundo. Rees could very well have received it, too. Feliciano unsurprisingly took Pitcher of the Year. He popped up, smiled, and accepted. This was a guy who last year played in the Major Leagues of Japan. He was the genuine article, the best pitcher in the league. It *should* have gone to him. Though my heart tugged in opposite directions, it was best to tip my cap. I was a sportsman, after all. I had character, integrity. I had a plaque.

38 *Yalla*

I WAS GOING HOME. IT HAD BEEN DIFFICULT TO SAY good-bye to my new friends. Standing outside the dorms of the *kfar*, waiting to pile into overstuffed vans, it was like a wedding, or a funeral. Guys assembled to offer their final words (though the peacocks were mysteriously absent). I saw Frankie first, and he wished me luck, said I could go play with him in the Colombian winter league.

"*A tu tambien*, Frankie. *Buena suerte*."

Unfortunately, Brito was nowhere to be found. Neither was Crabb, though Wiggy stood nearby. The Aussie seemed oddly reserved, the first time all summer he was not possessed of boundless energy. He looked *faklempt*. "All right, mate."

"All right, Wiggy." There was a pause.

"You know I'm coming to the States with my girl. San Fran is on our list."

"With a girl? You got a girlfriend?"

"Yeah, mate. Never told you?"

"No—I think you conveniently forgot."

"Maybe so," he said wryly.

To my surprise and satisfaction, Wiggy was true to his word. He would arrive at my doorstep, lithe young woman in tow, in the not-so-distant future.

Levy approached and we hugged, patting each other on the back. Conservative or not, we were boys. He lived in Los Angeles, so we promised to see each other soon. We would. Aside from being added to his right-wing Listserv, this was a good thing.

Then from Hastings, a firm, muscular embrace. He was my first friend in Israel. I thought about the initial morning in the caf, nervous, not knowing a soul, when I had seen him. How odd that he was also a teacher. Given our similar circumstances, I confided in him the night before about my upcoming decision. However, our talk only made things more difficult. It would take nearly a year, but we would meet again on the East Coast, near the Atlantic.

Then Fish. "I don't feel like this is the end," he said.

"I hope not. Who are we going to talk about Ramallah with?"

"No one's gonna believe our story." Fish hated good-byes and had a personal vendetta against clichés, so I threw some in, trying to lighten the mood.

He chuckled, motioned as if he had something to say, then stopped. We hugged once more. Though close in spirit, Fish and I would communicate most often via text messages, usually late on Friday and Saturday nights. He would tell me about some crazy escapade in Queens or the Bronx, and I would attempt to make up a cool story about my life. Maybe we would meet up, maybe not.

Rothem and I said our piece the previous night at *La Bomba*, hanging around the gas station. He was visibly upset by the season's conclusion. He had to return to full-time work and rec-league baseball. Back to real life, Dan was devastated. But he would visit me in San Francisco, officially on business.

It was not easy saying good-bye. These were my brothers. In a matter of months we had formed a special bond, a fraternity. As ballplayers, however, the thick air of emotion and sentiment was slightly unnerving, so I tried to cut the tension. "I'm not gonna get all choked up and emotional," I sassed. "I've got too much character, too much integrity. I'm a sportsman. You're looking at a major award winner."

"We call that the Kiss Ass Award."

"Sorry I didn't win Defensive Infielder of the Year, Fish. And sorry I didn't win Oldest Outfielder, Hastings. And sorry I'm not a conservative pundit, Levy." I got punched several times before piling into the van and waving at my buddies.

"*Yalla*, Prib."

"*Yalla*, bitches."

Pulling away, I pondered the word. *Yalla*. It meant many things: come on, let's go, good-bye. We used it during games, in the caf, around town. The refrain of our summer, *yalla* was an Arabic word adopted by Israelis. More fancifully, I thought, the expression might illustrate the possibility of a shared existence among peoples, the notion that the lives of Palestinians and Israelis could blend, mix. Maybe it starts with language and food, *yalla* and hummus, and maybe it continues through baseball. As Nelson Mandela famously noted, sport has the power to change the world. It has the power to unite people in a way that little else does. In any case, we had made *yalla* our own.

We drove south to Ben-Gurion Airport, bags stacked high in the beat-up gray van. I sat shotgun; others were in back. They talked about the league's chances for success, if it would last, discussed if they would ever come back to play. They talked about conquests and exploits, the parties, the crazy times. Somebody mentioned his brother was arrested back home for selling blow to an undercover agent in a nightclub. Not wholly part of the conversation, straining to hear, and having difficulty interjecting, I turned around to stare out the window.

Initially unconvinced of my faith, I realized I was leaving a changed man, a Jew assured of his heritage, more confident of his place in the world. Not a half-assed Jew, not kind of Jewish, and most certainly not a Five. Let some ticket lady interrogate me now. "You mean, am I Jewish?" I'd respond. "Absolutely." Similarly unsure of my physical abilities, I had also proved to myself that I could still pitch, still compete at a high level, if only in this exotic league. My average fastball, irregular slider, and decent change had carried me either to the end of the road or to the beginning of a much longer journey.

I thought of my conversation with Martin earlier that morning. The two of us sitting on a bench outside the caf, he said he needed an answer, that if I couldn't pitch they had to find someone else. But I couldn't make up my mind. Or didn't want to. I was afraid of being drunk on our whimsical season, this enchanting land. It was all such a bizarre reality. I was a teacher after all, this summer merely a reverie of years past. But what a beautiful reverie it had been, what a way to relaunch a career. I told him I had to wait until at least setting foot on American soil. After a sobering plane ride and talk with my family, a day tops, I would let him know. If he needed to make a decision before then, I would understand.

Otis Spann, Jack Johnson, Jimmie Cliff sang to me through tiny earbuds. What of this curious season—was it really all that special, and would it endure? I thought about bus rides into Tel Aviv and bus rides home from games. I thought about listening to records with DJ King Fish, sharing teaching stories with Jeff, arguing with Levy, learning from Rothem, watching El Ave turn the smoothest of double plays. If baseball were to succeed in Israel, it would be due to the people, not the publicity, the operating budget, or the revenue-sharing scheme. Baseball would succeed because *people* wanted to see Hastings crash into outfield walls, Pupo hit monster bombs, and Fish snag unreachable line drives at the corner. It would be because kids who at times pestered us indignantly for baseballs also chased fouls down the right-field line, clenching them in white-knuckled fists, refusing to let go, sleeping with the ball under their arms, dreaming of diving catches and triumphant strike threes. I thought of our young batboy, Yotam, whose first English word was *fuck*, learned most certainly from our blasphemous dugout. Yotam, who could not speak the language but was fluent in baseball. I thought about the two little boys in Palestine, playing catch a few miles away, a world apart. And I thought of Rothem being too stubborn and too proud to admit that in the end this season really *was* a dream come true.

Still in the van, I watched the night grow newly dark. Out the window a rising moon caught my eye. It was bold, crescent shaped, hanging just out of reach of the sun's fading amber glow, nestled securely in the graded blue twilight. All around it shone a surfeit of Hebrew stars, numerous and bright. They seemed to dance around the Muslim moon, deceptively unconnected yet tied to each other by the powerful force of the sun, an inverse portrait of life on the ground.

We drove into the night, and into the future. I remembered the rumor that the Kingdom of Jordan was starting a league. Whatever my decision, there was always next summer.

Epilogue

I'M NERVOUS. BUTTERFLIES FLUTTER IN MY STOMACH, running into one another, frenziedly bouncing off the walls of my abdomen. There is a big crowd, and I'm under the spotlight, the center of attention once again. It's hot, stuffy. I tug awkwardly at the shirt weighing heavily against my clavicle. My palm is sweaty, and I wipe it against the left hip of my pants, searching for the tacky sensation at the tips of my fingers. Standing as I've done so many times, feet shoulder-width apart, legs bent, I wonder if I have made the right decision. Much is at stake, trading one career for another.

Excitement mixes with regret, but there is no turning back. My mind is made up. Taking a deep breath, I look forward and begin: "What's up, class? Good morning. Nice to see everybody."

I shift my weight slightly on the hard surface. "I'm Mr. Pribble, and this is World Cultures. Hopefully, you're in the right place. Your first class of your first day of high school—pretty exciting. We're gonna have a good semester, but let's start with today."

I deliver the "who is Mr. Pribble" spiel, beginning with my attendance at a neighboring high school, continue through my years in Hawaii, my time in the South and the South of France, and finish with my teaching experience at Tam. As I speak I am unaware that Rafi Bergstrom will pitch for the Bridgeport Bluefish of the Atlantic League, becoming the first IBL player to sign a professional contract, instead of myself. I do not know that Jason Rees and Eladio Rodriguez will sign with the Yankees, that Maximo Nelson will sign with the Chunichi Dragons of Japan, that Juan Feliciano will turn down triple-A offers from three separate Major League teams in order to play in Mexico. And I have no idea there will never again be another Israel Baseball League, that but for a fleeting moment professional baseball bloomed in the desert, only to wither into the dust. Still talking, I point to the photos of my brother playing basketball at Cal, a hanging ukulele, and a Kokua Festival poster behind me to the right, asking forgiveness ahead of time for non sequiturs and tangents about two of my favorite things: Hawaii and my little brother. It's supposed to be a joke.

The thirteen and fourteen year olds are staring right at me, and the spotlight is shining bright. A couple of them laugh. There are some smiles and cheerful faces, some confused looks, and a smattering of kids feigning attention. I've got to tell them *something* about this summer, I think. But what exactly? I look down and notice I'm wearing a dress shirt rather than a jersey, loafers instead of spikes. At my feet there is no dirt, just linoleum. In my hand is a pen, not a baseball. And it's the first time I've had a close shave in months.

There are thirty young faces staring at me, but I'm all alone. I think back twenty-four hours and eight thousand miles, and I laugh. I was Prib for the past two months, a baseball player, an avatar of my youth. Now instead of baseballs I will sign hall passes; rather than asking for my autograph, kids will request to use the bathroom. It is at once normal and utterly foreign. I'm scared by the acknowledgment that such a transformation has come this easily. I am, once again, Mr. Pribble.

"And for the past two months I played baseball in Israel," I announce to the room. "It was f—." I stop myself. My lips catch what my mind intends to speak. You can't say *fuck* in the classroom, I remember. "It was fu— . . . fun." I think of a long-haired third baseman, a slender Yemenite beauty, a light pole in right field, a wild Australian, Ramallah, a camel, a near strike, schnitzel. The images are swirling in my mind, blending together abstractly. All at once I feel excited, happy, sad, angry, anxious, exhilarated, nostalgic. My thoughts and emotions tumble incoherently, and I realize I cannot do the story justice. "Um, maybe I'll tell you about it someday."

I am hours removed, and already it feels like a different life, a cruel mirage. Perhaps it was. Pangs of regret all too easily submerge beneath the comforting feeling of the classroom. We begin to go over the syllabus and discuss rules and procedures, grading, course content. Since this is World Cultures and Geography, I tell them, we will be looking at Africa, Latin America, Asia, Polynesia, and the Middle East, completing a peace project for the latter. I say that I'm passionate about this place, that what happens there impacts the world at large in a significant way. I tell them they will analyze a salient issue, such as the war in Afghanistan or the conflict in Israel and Palestine, and strive to find a solution. This may seem to be a difficult if not impossible task, yes, but that does not preclude the importance of such effort. Though some of the smartest and most influential people across the globe have been working on these issues for years, even ordinary individuals such as themselves can make a difference.

Things begin to loosen, to flow, both students and teacher finding the rhythm of the classroom. I cautiously foreshadow tales of visiting places previously referred to as war zones, eating hummus for breakfast, and playing baseball in the middle of the desert. To finish, we perform an icebreaker called Six Degrees of Me. I discover there are several avid horseback riders, two Muslims, a few guitarists, a handful of Jews, some athletes, an actor, and an aspiring politician. I steal a glance at the clock, see we have about a minute remaining, and make one last pitch. "Okay, everyone, nice work. We're gonna have a wonderful semester. Remember to get supplies and have your folks sign the syllabus. I hope you have a great first day of school, and I'll see you tomorrow. Peace in the Middle East. *Yalla*, bye."

Acknowledgments

THANKS TO MY MOM, LINI, FOR HER LOVE, PERSISTENT support, and encouragement. Self-esteem is the greatest gift a mother can give her son. To my dad, Jack, for his wisdom, sharp eye, and inspiration; everything I do in this world is to make him proud. And to my brother, Alex, for being a sounding board, a source of strength, and the greatest of friends.

I am deeply indebted to Russell Hill for his determined suggestion that I keep a journal in Israel, for his sage advice during the many stages of the manuscript, and for convincing me of my ability to tell this story. Also to my uncle Stephan Bodian for helping frame the manuscript and craft an engaging pitch.

I am forever grateful to Rob Taylor and the entire team at the University of Nebraska Press for believing in my story and for guiding this rookie with seasoned care. I would also like to thank Rick Brandon for his business savvy and relentless support, Cathryn Ramin for her incisive initial revisions, and Annette Wenda for her sensitive, expert copyediting skills. For invaluable industry advice, I owe a debt of gratitude to agents Jen Rofe and John Willig. For generously agreeing to include his photographs in this book I am indebted to Jacob Levy, and for his perspicacious feedback on all things political, cultural, and historical, I owe an equally large debt of gratitude to Dan Rothem.

Finally, thanks to the IBL management team for creating this impossible league, to those workers who made it tick, and, most important, to the players for their humor, competitive spirit, and eternal resilience. To those I have forgotten, to the countless others who have shared their thoughts, please accept as an apology my deeply felt Jewish guilt.

Pribble, Aaron,
1980-

Pitching in the
promised land.